Secrets of

Contemporary Slack Key Guitar

An Innovative Approach to Hawaiian Fingerstyle

AF702420

Daniel Ho
& Steve Sano

With a foreword by George Kahumoku Jr.

Alfred

ISBN 0-7390-1236-3 (Book & CD)

Cover photo © Stockbyte
Acoustic guitar courtesy of Martin Guitar

Table of Contents

Track 1

The CD that accompanies this book can make learning easier and more enjoyable. The symbol above will appear next to every example that is on the CD. Use the CD to help insure that you are capturing the feel of the examples, interpreting the rhythms correctly, and so on. The track numbers below the symbols correspond directly to the examples on that page. Track 1 is an introduction to the CD.

Foreword

It is said that out of adversity comes opportunity. In April of 1998, I was asked by Uncle Ray & Aunty Elodia Kāne to accompany them on a California concert tour. At the time, Uncle's health was declining and the promoters were afraid that if he got sick and couldn't perform, the concerts would have to be cancelled. As God would have it, Uncle was perfectly well, but it was Aunty Elodia who developed an ear infection and couldn't make the trip. Without Aunty Elodia, Uncle couldn't travel.

There was a big scramble to find a replacement for Uncle. The promoters felt that another person was needed besides my son Keoki, Patrick Landeza and me to round out the show. The search was now on! Hawaiian slack key guitarists considered included Led Kaapana, Cyril Pahinui, Dennis Kamakahi, and Pekelo Cosma. However, due to scheduling and previous commitments none of them were available. On the recommendation of my great friend the hula dancer, Leilani Marino of Santa Rosa, California, and after several prayers, I took a chance and called Daniel Ho to see if he was available. Daniel said that he could rearrange his schedule and that it would be an honor to join us on the tour. This was the beginning of our slack key relationship.

One of the qualities I admired about Daniel was his easy going "local boy" manner, his humility and humbleness. When I listened to his music, I heard the same thread that tied all of us *kī hō'alu* (slack key) players together, the *nahenahe* (soft, sweet, and soothing) music of Hawai'i. What made Daniel's music unique however, was his ability to play sweet single notes with repeating themes and the honesty of his work. We completed a successful tour and talked of doing an album together.

It was suggested that it would be great to have an album of Hawaiian hymns. Daniel knew the hymns but not the Hawaiian lyrics. What Daniel didn't know was that in 1986 my grandmother, Emily Ho'opale Dulay, had asked me to do an album of her favorite Hawaiian hymns, so I had collected and researched over 200 hymns. With the help of Kekepa Lee and Danny Palakiko, Sr., I chose my *tutu's* (grandmother's) favorite hymns and recorded them with Daniel in 1999. We named the album *Hymns of Hawai'i.* It was the culmination of our first collaboration. This CD won a Nā Hōkū Hanohano Award in May 2000 for Best Religious Album of the Year.

Daniel and I traveled extensively together promoting Hymns of Hawai'i. In Phoenix, Arizona, I saw first hand the brilliancy and creativity of Daniel's mind when he shared his tunings and how he arrived at them with a slack key class that we both taught at the Aloha Festival. There are many schools of thought and methods of learning. I learned the traditional Hawaiian way, which was to observe *(ho'onana),* to listen *(ho'olohe),* to mimic *(ho'opili)* and mostly *ho'o kulikuli waha* (to shut your mouth and ask no questions). Daniel's approach was totally formal and musically astounding to me because not only could he play his music, he could also notate it for future reference so that he could recall it when needed. My method was to memorize the music and words and share them by playing the songs. The disadvantage of this method, I am finding out, is that sometimes the memory fails. For example, I have several songbooks of lyrics from my dad, my grandparents, and my great grandparents, however, I've forgotten the *na ea* or *na leo* (melodies). When I listened to Daniel explain his slack key method I saw in my mind's eye all the possibilities and advantages of learning his method, especially in the areas of composition and song writing. It is my wish that those who embrace Daniel's innovative approach to the traditional style of slack key take the best from both worlds and continue to maintain the *nahenahe* thread that *na hilo* (weaves) us together.

At my third annual Hawaiian slack key guitar workshop held on Maui in June 2000, I was able to observe more intimately Daniel Ho's approach to teaching Hawaiian slack key. I found that his greatest asset is his ability to offer yet another way for others to learn, to notate, and become more creative with their music. It is my hope and prayer that this book will be a gift and a blessing to all who love Hawaiian music.

George Kahumoku, Jr.
Lahaina, Maui, Hawai'i
June 29, 2000

Daniel Ho

Preface

My purpose for writing this book is to share some interesting revelations I've discovered in my studies of slack key guitar. In this book we'll discuss a set of criteria you can use to develop your own original tunings. We'll also study the G Kilauea tuning, a versatile tuning for solo slack key guitar I developed through this process.

It is a great honor for me that Steve Sano would impart his vast knowledge of *kī hō'alu* in this book. He has taught me important lessons about a performer's responsibility to composers and audiences, and a teacher's responsibility to facts, history, and students. I trust you will find his well-researched, well-documented chapters free from bias and engagingly informative. Steve and I were also blessed with the talents of his literally "in-house" editor in chief, his wife, Linda Uyechi. Thank you, Linda!

I hope you find this book helpful in your quest to understand and perform this wonderful art form, and that the process brings you many rewarding hours of fun and discovery.

Aloha,

Daniel Ho

If you have any questions or comments as you work through this book, please e-mail me at:

Daniel@DanielHo.com

Dedication

This book is dedicated to my father, Arthur Ho, who's love and unconditional support of my irrational ambition as a youth helped me to enjoy this rewarding profession as an adult.

Acknowledgements

I'd like to thank my father who paid for my organ, ukulele, classical guitar, piano, drums, music theory, bass, dance, and voice lessons, drove me to and from the lessons, and dealt with years of aggravating noise as I practiced incessantly! I'd like to thank my wife, Teresa, who has been nothing but supportive of me, my daughter, Lia, who is my joy and inspiration, Steve Harder who made this book possible, Steve Sano for sharing his wealth of knowledge and co-authoring this book, Linda Uyechi for her editing expertise, George Kahumoku, Jr. for opening my eyes to the world of slack key, Frank Paul, Larry Lingle, and Jean Larrivée Guitars Ltd. for the world's greatest guitars, and Ron Manus and everyone at Alfred Publishing for believeing in us! Special thanks also to Dean Taba, Nick Mitsakos, Keith Hiraoka, Ed and Helen Bigelow, and Paul and Sandy Konwiser.

Biography

Daniel Ho was born and raised in Kaimukī, a small town on the island of O'ahu. From 1990–1997, Daniel was the leader, keyboardist, producer, and composer for the contemporary jazz group Kilauea. They released six best selling smooth jazz albums reviewed as "some of the finest, most popular and melodic contemporary jazz music available."

His debut solo record, *Watercolors,* is a blend of Daniel's classic contemporary jazz sound infused with highlights of Hawaiian slack key guitar. It was during the making of this record that he realized his interest in slack key guitar, a style he only briefly touched upon as a youth. As a result, Daniel recorded *The Voyage Home,* a Hawaiian-style slack key guitar album of classic Hawaiian music and a few original compositions. Shortly after meeting slack key master, George Kahumoku, Jr., on a 1999 tour of California, Daniel and George collaborated on *Hymns of Hawai'i,* a collection of Hawai'i's most famous hymns sung in Hawaiian by George. It won the coveted *Nā Hōkū Hanohano* Award for Religious Album of the Year 2000. Daniel's second slack key record, *Beyond Blue,* expands the limits of slack key guitar by introducing saxophones, flutes and percussion to the mix. *Beyond Blue* includes a koto/slack key duet with June Kuramoto of Hiroshima on a piece entitled *Sacred Journey.*

Steve Sano

Preface

Years ago, I learned a lesson I've never forgotten. Kenny Endo, a master North American taiko performer, shared a lesson that he learned from his teacher: whenever one performs, it may be the first time a listener experiences the art form—or it may be the last.

What this means is that a performer shoulders special responsibilities—first, to the memory of those who have played before, and second, to those listening. The first responsibility is to acknowledge the cultural and aesthetic base that masters of the art form create, and to which the performer is indebted. With that realization, the second responsibility is to share the art form responsibly—bearing in mind the need to understand not only its technical nuances but also its cultural and spiritual heritage.

In short, it's all about respect.

As a non-Hawaiian, a musician trained in classical western European music, and a third-generation Japanese American whose being is rooted in respect, this is the lesson that allows me to pursue my studies of *kī hō'alu.* I believe that to approach a tradition as an outsider requires extra sensitivity to the issues of culture, history, community, and identity inherent in that art form. It is impossible for me to live my life over as Hawaiian, but I can approach my studies with a "beginner's mind," an open attitude towards every experience that allows me to absorb new ideas, to explore new perspectives, and to rediscover and re-examine familiar ideas in every lesson.

In every teacher there is a student; in every lesson, there is something new to be learned. It is in this spirit that I offer my contributions here—always looking forward to sharing ideas, and always learning from the lessons that emerge.

Aloha,

Steve Sano

Acknowledgements

Mahalo to Daniel Ho for his outstanding musicianship and the opportunity to collaborate on this project; to the faculty and staff at the Stanford University Department of Music; to the folks at Gryphon Stringed Instruments for their support; to George "Keoki" Winston for the wealth of material on *kī hō'alu* that he so generously shares with the slack key community; to Susan Kanagawa for her creative artistry and for sharing the love of her Island home with me; to the many students who have shared bits of Hawai'i in Stanford's *kī hō'alu* seminar; to Keola and Moanalani Beamer, George Kahmoku, Jr., and Ozzie Kotani, who, by sharing the spirit and music of Hawai'i during their visits to Stanford inspire all who experience their art, and to my family and all the aunties and uncles in the Islands for their hospitality whenever I visit! Big mahalos especially to Ozzie: kumu, mentor, and most of all, friend. And of course, to Linda — my partner in words, music, and life.

Biography

Conductor, Director of Choral Studies and Associate Professor of Music at Stanford University, Steve discovered his connection to the music of Hawai'i years ago when he was drawn to the innovative *kī hō'alu* style of Ozzie Kotani. Steve began studying with the slack key master and Ozzie's deep respect and love for the art form touched Steve's own reverence for musical traditions. Through the years, Ozzie's artistry has continued to inspire Steve's exploration of *kī hō'alu.*

Steve supports the art form at Stanford by inviting slack key artists to campus and by teaching a seminar that places slack key in its historical, social, cultural, and political context. Keenly aware of his off-island origins, Steve continues to approach his relationship to slack key with the care and responsibility he believes is demanded of all practitioners but particularly those who approach it from outside the Island community. Acknowledging the powerful spirit of those who have gone before him, Steve's goal is to always approach the art form and its masters with the greatest reverence and respect. It is his hope that all students of slack key share these sensibilities, creating a community of players worthy of the powerful Hawaiian roots of *kī hō'alu.*

Chapter 1

Kī hō'alu: The New Renaissance of a Hawaiian Musical "Tradition"

"Tradition"—such a slippery term! After all, "traditions" constantly change, evolve, are re-defined, and of course, are "broken." As with many musics rooted in the folk idiom, *kī hō'alu* is experiencing a wide-ranging renaissance both within and beyond the community where it originated. As an outgrowth of this current popularity, the "tradition" of *kī hō'alu* is being impacted by all manner of influence from outside the cradle of Hawaiian music. Even a cursory sampling of recently produced slack key recordings reveals the prominent influence of other musics: jazz, Latin, Celtic, not to mention contemporary fingerstyle guitar—which itself reflects myriad cultural and musical influences. In addressing the issue of "tradition," it would seem that we need to consider the influences already evident in the progressing evolution of the art form, while at the same time maintaining an awareness of and a sensitivity to the history and pre-existing forms of the genre.

In short, *kī hō'alu* is evolving into areas that many master performers may not recognize as Hawaiian slack key guitar. This begs the question "*what is slack key?*" Certainly, there are salient characteristics that can be identified in older styles of playing: recognized tunings, alternating bass patterns, characteristic melodic or harmonic formulas or vamps, and a common repertoire. But, how many of these characteristics are "required" to define a piece as "slack key"? Where is the line between *kī hō'alu* and a style of playing that would otherwise be described simply as fingerstyle guitar?

Perhaps, as with other genres of contemporary music, the time has come for the broad category of slack key to be sub-divided into more specific categories. Just as "rock music" serves as a cover term for a variety of styles, identified as classic rock, surf rock, heavy metal, speed metal, ska, and such, "slack key" might be regarded as a cover term for sub-categories such as old-style slack key, contemporary slack key, or progressive slack key.

In addition, there is the issue of pedagogy. With whom has one studied? Does one's playing reflect the style of their teacher? If a person is self-taught, what influences are present in their playing? Granted, there are no easy answers to these questions. Indeed, as *kī hō'alu* experiences an increasingly accelerated evolution, the defining characteristics themselves become less defined.

One of the wonderful things about any musical form is its ability to evolve and grow. As an art form gains increasingly wider acceptance, external influences are bound to proliferate. However, even as an art form evolves, one must always be aware of its roots. In this climate of *kī hō'alu*'s ever-expanding domains, comprehensive training in the art form demands knowledge of and fluency in a broad range of recognized styles, tunings, and repertoire. In this respect, players of this style of music are always students—an enviable position when one considers the richness of the learning process.

This book explores only one part of the *kī hō'alu* genre—a part progressive enough in style that its inclusion as "slack key" may even push the envelope of its definition! In reflecting upon the evolving nature of the genre, the style presented here is representative of one direction the art form is going.

Hence, a word to the wise is appropriate here: To experience the richness of *kī hō'alu*, learn the materials in this book, but don't stop here! Search out other published teaching materials. Attend workshops given by master teachers. Seek out private instruction from leading players fluent in a wide range of styles, both old and new. Listen often to recordings by master performers and to a variety of artists. Only then, can you start to fully appreciate the range and complexity of this beautiful musical "tradition."

Chapter 2

TOWARD A BRIEF HISTORY OF KĪ HŌ'ALU

King Kamehameha III

The most common story of the genesis of Hawaiian slack key guitar is by now legend—it's told in countless liner notes and concert programs, on stage and in workshops. In a 1974 interview on Hawai'i Public Television, Auntie Alice Namakelua, one of the great old style *kī hō'alu* performers and teachers, recalled that in 1832 *vaqueros,* cowboys from Mexico, traveled to the Big Island of Hawai'i at the request of King Kamehameha III. They were needed to help manage the cattle that were a gift from Captain George Vancouver to the Hawaiian royalty in 1793 and 1794. Over the years, the cattle had proliferated and the Hawaiians needed help bringing the foreign stock under control.

Besides their livestock expertise—and of greater interest to us here—the *vaqueros* brought guitars with them. So the *paniolo,* Hawaiian cowboys, not only received lessons in cattle management, they also broadened their cultural horizons. When the *vaqueros* completed their term contracts and returned to Mexico, they left behind their guitars—or so the story goes—for the *paniolo* to inherit and adapt to their own musical style and repertoire.

Though this story is embedded in *kī hō'alu* lore, it's not necessarily the final word. For example, ethnomusicologist Elizabeth Tatar proposes that the guitar may have been introduced to Hawai'i as early as the late 1700's or early 1800's. In the long-out-of-print, but still highly regarded encyclopedia, *Hawaiian Music and Musicians,* Tatar notes that long before the arrival of the *vaqueros,* the guitar was popular in early America—and Hawai'i was a stopover for traders and whalers as well as a destination for missionaries. Putting two and two together, it's entirely plausible and, indeed, quite possible that the guitar was familiar to Hawaiians even as the cattle were lowing and their herd size was growing.

The missionaries arrived in 1820, and, as history records, music has always been one of the primary tools of Christianization and colonization of indigenous populations. The rich tradition of *hīmeni,* or hymn singing, is clear testament to this fact. In fact, as noted in *Hawaiian Music and Musicians,* the earliest recorded date of hymn singing in Honolulu is 23 April 1820. Given that the guitar is eminently portable, it is easy to imagine that a few instruments might have made their way over in the hands of the missionaries.

All that, plus Tatar raises the possibility that the Hawaiians themselves may have brought the guitar to the Islands. In 1818 King Kamehameha sent 80 Hawaiians to Monterey to fight for the army of Rio de la Plata (now Argentina). Why not posit that the Hawaiians, enchanted with the sound of the instrument, brought it back with them when they returned home?

Given the passage of time, the lack of eyewitnesses, and the scant inconclusive documentation, it is clear that no matter how the stories are told, they converge on a relatively brief period of time—the early 1800's. According to Tatar, the clincher for a terminus antiquem, or latest possible date for the introduction of the guitar to Hawai'i, is an advertisement by the Henry Paty Company of Honolulu, dated 6 June 1840, in which guitar strings are listed for sale. At the least, by the summer of 1840, guitar owners formed a viable consumer group in Hawai'i. The rest, as they say, is history.

Or, rather, evolution. No matter how Hawaiians linked up with the guitar, it is clear that the connection was serendipitous. The music they produced seems at times magical—yet slack key is firmly grounded in reality. Hawaiian song, chant, and dance provided fertile ground for the development of a new genre of fingerstyle guitar playing.

Take, for example, one of the most basic components of "traditional" old style slack key, the alternating bass. Its rhythmic underpinnings are drawn from the *mele hula,* a form of chant accompanied by dance. A typical recording of *mele hula* such as the chant *Mele inoa no Hi'iaka; hula kuahu* (from *Nā Leo Hawai'i Kahiko: The Master Chanters of Hawai'i/Songs of Old Hawai'i,* Mountain Apple Company, MACD 2043), reveals the characteristic kāhela or kāholo pattern of the *pahu* (shark-skin headed drum) or *'ipu* (gourd drum). The song syllabary for the rhythmic pattern is *pā pa'i, pā pa'i.* Here it is in western notation (Fig. 4.1):

Fig. 2.1

With this in mind, consider a slack key piece in the "traditional" style. Ozzie Kotani's teaching piece *Kani Kī hō'alu* is a great example *(Kani Kī hō'alu,* Dancing Cat Records 08022 38013-2). Note carefully the way the alternating bass interacts with the melody. There's no mistaking the haunting, hypnotic rhythm of the *mele hula.*

Of course, the most salient characteristic of slack key is simultaneously melodic and harmonic: the use of altered, or *scordatura* tuning. The term *scordatura* is derived from the Italian, *scordare,* meaning to "mistune." No one has yet stepped forward with a proposal for precisely when the first Island tuning emerged, nor given the folk origins of the tradition and the unavailability of recorded sound in the late-18th and early-19th centuries, is anyone likely to. Scholars and other interested people do, however, ponder why altered tunings may have formed the basis for this uniquely Hawaiian genre of fingerstyle guitar.

Some posit that tunings may have been altered to accommodate an individual's vocal range. Others assume that, in the absence of formal lessons, altered tunings were the "natural" initial response of a novice seeking easily playable and pleasing harmonies.

Thus is the basis for *kī hō'alu*—the introduction of a versatile instrument to the music-rich Hawaiian culture, the incorporation of familiar rhythmic patterns, and the development of tunings well suited to the repertoire and aesthetic sensibilities of a musically prolific island people.

Evolution and Authenticity

The subsequent evolution of the slack key style has included influences from many diverse musics. The recent revolution in popularity of slack key has resulted not only in rapid dissemination of recorded music but also in rapid growth of the playing community. The days of sharing slack key styles and secrets through the backyard *kani ka pila* (literally, to play music, though in local vernacular, a jam session), and then only with one's *'ohana* or family (blood and/or extended) are passing quickly.

The commercial success of slack key is a double-edged sword: once-closely-held styles of slack key will now live longer than their masters, but the stories, culture, and family histories which accompanied them are no longer guaranteed partners to their musical expression. And as those styles move beyond the walls of the *kūpuna's* (elders') yards, they are changing rapidly.

Masters considered today to be "old style" or "traditional," play in a way that was considered "outside the tradition" by players of a previous generation. Auntie Alice Namakelua once described the playing style of a young performer as "not slack key". Hard to believe that those words were once used to describe one of today's most celebrated "traditional" style players!

In fact, a closer look at what today would be considered "traditional" style, shows ingenious incorporation of new with old. Consider the playing style of Ray Kāne. Though solidly grounded in a foundational alternating bass and, for the most part, utilizing primary harmonic construction (i.e. almost always only I, IV, and V chords or their functional substitutes), his work also reflects, as Tatar describes, the influence of Spanish and flamenco styles of guitar playing.

The work of this unquestionable master, imbued with the spirit of old Hawai'i and representing one of the bridges between the backyard *kani ka pila* and the modern recording studio, raises the question inevitable in a living folk art. What is "authentic"? What characterizes "real" slack key? And who will function as judge, labeling what is and what is not?

All folk art, particularly one with the humble beginnings of *kī hō'alu* and grassroots links to social and political issues is subject to this question. The easy answer is to disengage from careful contextualization of the art form and to take it only at its musical face value. The more considered response is to accept the responsibility to respect and honor the art form in as many dimensions as it is presented to us—to take seriously the value of "beginner's mind" as we become students of a folk art.

Being empowered with understanding, armed with compassion, and still enraptured by the sounds of *kī hō'alu* places members of the growing community of players and admirers in a better position to begin addressing questions of authenticity. Is it a stretch to accept today's styles and sounds as "real", albeit contemporary or progressive slack key?

We invite the reader to join us as we struggle to formulate a response to that question. The issue of authenticity is one that is simply too difficult to codify in a few words, pages, or conversations. We prefer to allow it to stand as an ever-present challenge—to spur ongoing thoughtful growth of each player and of the slack key community at large.

Perhaps the answers ultimately lie in the respect that the art form demands of all those that participate in its continued evolution. In that vein, we hope that players who imitate and innovate do so as they acknowledge the influences of the masters, and that composers who cast and recast, form and re-form, do so with the deliberateness that reflects a deep understanding and love for the art form. Finally, we hope that the music they play falls on the ears of listeners who are knowledgeable enough to recognize the reflections of respect in the music they embrace.

Chapter 3

Slack Key Tuning

"Slack" key? What's that? It's *kī hō'alu*—where *kī* refers to the guitar's tuning keys and *hō'alu* means to loosen or slacken.

The loosening or slackening of the keys provides the basic mechanics for many *kī hō'alu* tunings. In truth, the loosening or slackening is all relative. Specifically, it's relative to the "standard" western tuning of the guitar: E A D G B E. In one of the most common slack key tunings, G taro patch, three of the strings are lowered a whole step: the first-string "E" is lowered to "D", the fifth-string "A" is lowered to "G", and the sixth-string "E" is lowered to "D". The rest of the strings stay the same, resulting in the altered tuning of D G D G B D.

In technical terms, the slacking of the keys causes the distance between the first and second strings to be reduced from a perfect fourth to a minor third and the distance between the fourth and fifth strings to increase from a perfect fourth to a perfect fifth. The distance between the fifth and sixth strings remains constant at a perfect fourth, but the perfect fourth occurs a whole step lower than in standard tuning. Voilà—a G major chord! For the more visually inclined, *Fig. 3.1a and 3.1b* might make more sense.

Fig. 3.1a Track 2

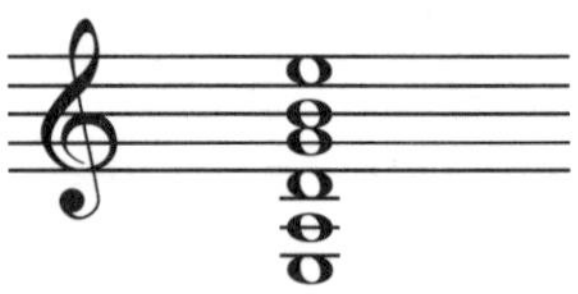

Standard Guitar Tuning

Fig. 3.1b Track 3

G Taro Patch Tuning

Simply put, this altered tuning results in a more "consonant", or pleasing, sound. Note that the term "consonant" is in quotes. Just as "slacking" the keys is a relative concept, so is the notion of consonance. What is music to your ears might not be pleasing to someone from another culture, place, or time.

Such was the case for the pre-European contact Hawaiians. Before the Europeans landed, Hawaiian musical tradition was primarily vocal, dominated by chant that reflected their own sense of aesthetics. Without going into great detail regarding the musical constructions of pre- and post-European contact Hawai'i, a quick look at examples from both genres of vocal styles, ancient and acculturated, shows the dramatic influences that the European concept of consonance had on the Hawaiian music scene.

The excerpt in *Fig. 3.2* illustrates the characteristics of unaccompanied pre-contact chant, *Mele Oli.* Although the transcription can't capture the microtonal variations in pitch or minute fluctuations in rhythm used to accommodate the natural speech rhythms of the Hawaiian language, it does show the limited range of pitch in this genre. Only two pitches are used. Here "C" is the principal recitation tone and the "A" a minor third below is the lower auxiliary tone. Rhythmically, there is little variety.

Fig. 3.2

Mele inoa no Hi'iaka; hula kuahu.
Name chant for the goddess Hi'iaka: formal dance.

The melody in *Fig. 3.3* illustrates the influences of European contact. This is one of Hawai'i's most famous melodies—Queen Lili'uokalani's *Ke Aloha O Ka Haku*, more commonly known as *The Queen's Prayer.* In this poignant melody, the Queen incorporated a number of European characteristics. The melody is constructed from a larger number of pitches across the range of a major 10th and is grounded in the key of C major. Rhythmically, common-time meter anchors the tune; structurally, it uses symmetrical two-bar phrases. Although by authorship, a Hawaiian song, *The Queen's Prayer* is clearly at least cousin to other European melodies of the day.

Fig. 3.3

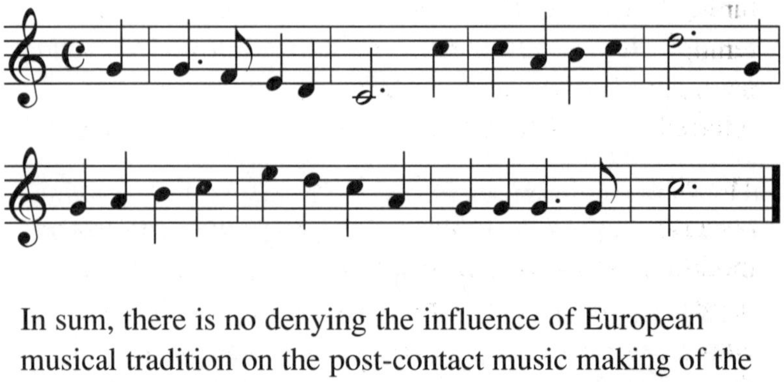

In sum, there is no denying the influence of European musical tradition on the post-contact music making of the Hawaiians. So it is little surprise that the "consonance"

of major chord tonality, a mainstay of western music since the late Renaissance, is reflected in many commonly recognized *kī hō'alu* tunings.

For example, one of the most comprehensive resources for *kī hō'alu* tunings, *Slack Key Tuning Essay* by George Winston, reveals a great number of tunings based on a major chord as the anchoring feature of a tuning's architecture. Winston lists eight tunings categorized as "Major" tunings, 25 tunings categorized as "*Wahine*" tunings (incorporating a raised seventh scale degree from the root), and eleven tunings as "*Mauna Loa*" tunings (incorporating the interval of a perfect fifth between the two highest sounding strings).

But before exploring more specific characteristics of *kī hō'alu* tunings, it is important to take a step back. Even though altered tunings are at the very heart of the art form, slack key players may not take sole credit for "discovering" altered tunings. Far from it! The tunings in *kī hō'alu* are actually part of a larger class of *scordatura* tunings, as mentioned in Chapter 2. These altered tunings are found in a diverse range of musics beyond the reefs of Hawai'i.

Scordatura tunings are used in both art music (in rough terms, "music for music's sake") and folk music (in even rougher terms, music for the common people). In art music, Mozart and Mahler are among many classical composers who have used altered tunings. For example, Mozart's *Sinfonia concertante*, K.V. 364 is composed in E-flat major; however, the solo viola part was originally notated in D major with the intention that the instrument be tuned one half-step higher than standard. In folk music, players from a variety of guitar traditions use altered tunings. Across the ocean in Samoa, the *kī hō'alu* tuning F G C G C E is also known as "Samoan C Major tuning." In the music scene on the North American continent, the *kī hō'alu* taro-patch (open G) tuning is also referred to as "G-tuning for dobro" or "Spanish Tuning."

The class of *scordatura* tuning is even more interesting because there are two different ways in which tunings are modified. In the first case, all the strings of an instrument are altered in the same direction and by the same amount, preserving the intervallic relationship between the strings. In other words, the distance between any given string and the ones adjacent to it remains constant. In the second case, the strings are altered in different amounts and possibly in different directions so that the intervallic relations between the strings are changed. The art music of Austrian romantic composer Gustav Mahler provides a nice example of the first type of *scordatura* tuning and the folk music of *kī hō'alu* provides a relevant example of the second.

In his *Fourth Symphony*, Mahler asks that the solo violin be provided with two instruments. One is to be tuned to the standard G D A E, and the second is to be in an altered tuning A E B F♯. It's easy to see in *Fig 3.4* that the only difference between the two tunings is that the altered version is a whole-step higher than the standard and that the intervallic relationship between any string and its neighbors remains perfect fifths.

Fig. 3.4

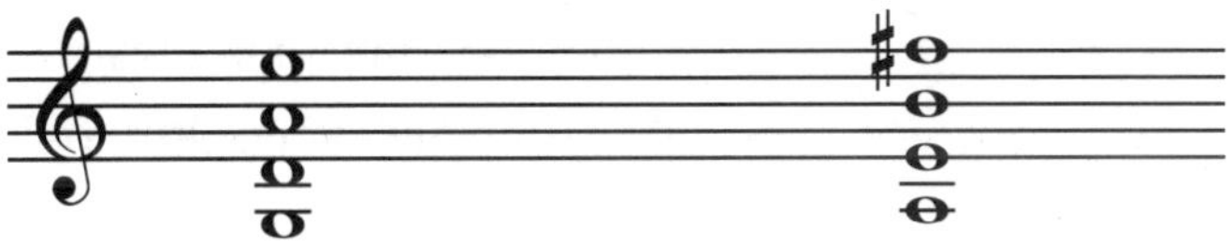

Standard Violin Tuning | *Altered Violin Tuning*

Moving from Mahler to *kī hō'alu*, recall that the change from standard to taro patch tuning required that three of the strings were lowered and three remained the same. In this case, the pitch relations between the strings are changed dramatically. Refer back to Fig. 3.1b for visual confirmation, and tune and re-tune your guitar for aural confirmation. The altered tunings for *kī hō'alu* provide a rich set of examples for the second type of *scordatura* tunings described above. This becomes even more evident as we move beyond taro patch tuning.

In fact, there is great diversity of character in the set of recognized tunings. As noted before, the major chord is a fundamental influence in *kī hō'alu* tunings, providing the basis for familiar "consonant" sounds. One example among many is "Atta's C" (C G E G C E), named after the late *kī hō'alu* master Atta Isaacs. Just like taro patch tuning, when strummed unfretted Atta's C produces an intuitively pleasing chord to the western ear. Other tunings based on a major chord may add a "color tone" such as a major seventh or major sixth, and produce similarly pleasing sounds.

But open string consonance is not the only characteristic of slack key tunings. Some tunings are aurally less intuitive, but musically quite clever. Take, for example, "Keola's C" (C G D G B E), named after *kī hō'alu* master Keola Beamer. When strummed unfretted, it doesn't sound as obviously "consonant" as taro patch or Atta's C. On closer examination, however, musically it's sensitive, sensible, and more complex. There are two ways to think of it's structure: either as incorporating elements of both G major and C major chords, or as a Cmaj9 chord. For the player, this structure is versatile and easily adapted to a variety of musical considerations. Similarly, Daniel's "G Kilauea" tuning introduced in the next chapter provides an aural puzzle with a pleasing musical resolution.

But before leaving a discussion of tunings, it's worth taking a closer look at one of the features of *kī hō'alu* directly impacted by these tunings.

Vamps: Slack Key Style

Vamps, or repeated cadential formulas (a cadence is a point at which the music comes to rest or resolution—it may be the end of a piece, the end of a verse, or even just the end of a phrase), are one of the most recognizable characteristics of slack key playing. The sound of a vamp alone is often enough to signal to the listener that it is Hawaiian music. For the seasoned *kī hō'alu* player the sound of a vamp can signal much more, as we will show.

Start by tuning your instrument to taro patch tuning (D G D G B D), then play the vamp in *Fig. 3.5*. There's no mistaking the characteristic sound of Hawaiian slack key guitar—even in those few notes.

Fig. 3.5 Track 4

For contrast, try the vamp in *Fig. 3.6*, but first tune to G *wahine* (D G D F♯ B D). This tuning is also referred to as "Double Slack", "Slack G Tuning" or "Namakelua's Tuning".

Fig. 3.6 Track 5

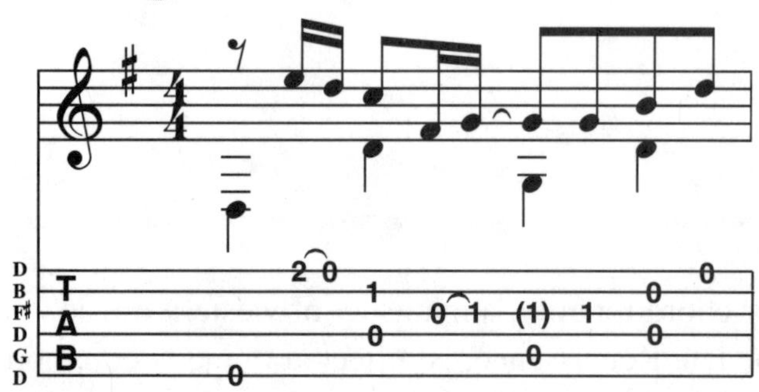

The visceral impact is still the same—it's slack key! But the musical impact is different—that's a whole different sound. In fact, many different tunings have their own characteristic vamps.

Vamps are characteristic of their tunings because the tuning itself creates pitch relationships between the strings which, along with the physical realities of the guitar, help shape the sound of a vamp. In other words, some patterns are simply easier to play in certain tunings. The best example of this is an example in futility: Keeping the sound of the G wahine vamp (*Fig. 3.6*) fresh in your ears, re-tune your guitar to taro patch and try to re-produce it. (Hint: Use the 4th string higher up on the fingerboard.) If at first you succeed, then "awkward" may be one of the more genteel words to fall from your lips. If you find the exercise impossible, don't despair. Simply tune to G *wahine.* Point made?

Hence, the large number of tunings and the equally large number of vamps in slack key playing are not accidents. Each vamp lends a characteristic sound to a given tuning. The greater the variety of tunings you learn, the greater the number of vamps you will discover. Conversely, the greater the variety of vamps you are familiar with will provide you with the ability to recognize a greater number of tunings.

That said, a final word to the beginner and the wise is in order.

When exploring different tunings, keep in mind one of the lessons from the master slack key artist and teacher Sonny Chillingworth as recalled by Ozzie Kotani. Sonny was fond of reminding his students that one of the signs of a good slack key player is not necessarily the number of tunings they can play, but rather the number of songs they could play in a single tuning! Having learned that lesson from Sonny himself, Ozzie's message is similar—one of the hallmarks of a developed player is their ability to "open up repertoire" in a tuning. By this he means being able to develop and demonstrate fluency, creativity, and artistry across a broad range of repertoire within a single tuning.

One of the allures of slack key may be the technical opportunities it opens up with its vast range of alternative tunings. But at the heart of the music is still the spirit and sensibilities of the masters. Enjoy it all!

Chapter 4

Finding Your Own Slack Key Tuning

As we explore the nature of slack key and the unique characteristics of various tunings, let's discuss how you can discover some tunings of your own. Literally, there are 2,985,984 different tunings to choose from (12^6 = 2,985,984).

The best way to find a tuning that works for you is to sit down with seven gallons of Kona coffee (you'll need this to keep you awake during this process), buy 88 sets of strings (you'll probably break 87 of the 88 sets—the 88th set is so you can enjoy your newfound tuning), and start experimenting with each of these tunings until you happen upon one with which you connect emotionally. NOT! An easier approach might be to use the following six considerations as an aid: tension, key, open strings, melody, counterpoint and chords, and bass.

Tension

A guitar functions optimally in standard tuning: E, A, D, G, B, E. The scale length, fret placement, action, bracing, truss rod, and body size are all designed to maximize tone, intonation, and playability at these pitches. When you tighten and/or loosen strings, the delicate balance of the guitar is disrupted. The intonation starts to suffer, the action becomes either too low, causing strings to buzz against the frets, or too high, making the guitar difficult to play. When choosing your pitches, it is probably best to not exceed a minor third below the standard pitch of a string, or a major second above. Though not necessary, a possible strategy might be to raise some pitches above the standard tuning and lower others below. This will keep the overall tension of the guitar strings similar to that for which it was designed.

Key

The key of your tuning might be based upon either a major or minor tonality. The tonal center of your key may be determined by other musicians or vocalists with whom you perform. If you are a soloist and the key is entirely your decision, consider the tension of your strings and how it will affect your piece. For example, if you're playing an up-tempo piece in G taro patch, you might want to tune a half step higher to G♯. This will put three strings above standard tuning and three strings below, will increase the tension relative to G tuning and might give you a brighter, snappier sound. If you're playing a slow ballad primarily in first position and would like a broader sound, try tuning your G taro patch down a half step to F♯. You are still not more than a minor third away from standard tuning and the looser tension and lower pitches may give you a warmer sound.

Open Strings

When it comes right down to it, one of the primary reasons we use alternate tunings is to increase the number of open strings available to us. When your left hand is not required to finger many pitches, bar chords, etc., it is free to play more interesting and intricate parts with greater ease. Open strings also contribute to a rich tone full of sympathetic vibrations and overtones that are not as prominent when strings are fretted.

For example, play the following two examples and listen to the difference. Fig 4.1 is a first-position E major chord in standard tuning. Three strings are fretted and three strings are open.

Fig. 4.1 Track 6

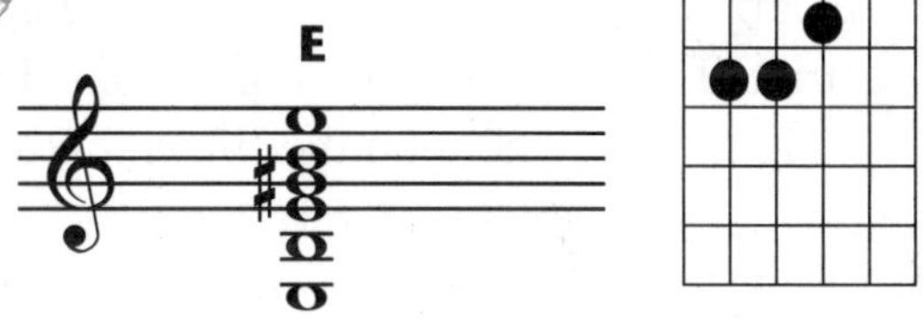

Fig. 4.2 is an F major chord in standard tuning barred at the first fret—none of the strings are open.

Fig. 4.2 Track 7

Which sounds fuller? Which sounds richer? Which sustains longer?

Another parallel could be drawn to the piano and its sustain pedal (also called the damper pedal). When you depress a key on an acoustic piano, depending on the pitch, a felt hammer hits one, two or three strings a split second after the damper is lifted off the string. If you first depress the sustain pedal with your foot, then play that very same key, the sound will be much richer. Why? Because the sustain pedal lifts the dampers off every string, not just the ones being played. This allows all the strings in the piano to vibrate sympathetically, creating rich overtones around the pitch being played. A similar phenomenon is observable on the guitar. If you pluck the low E string without touching any of the other strings, you will hear them all resonate sympathetically. Now try muting all the strings with your left hand while plucking just the low E string with your right hand. How does the sound change?

Melody, Counterpoint/Chords, and Bass

In solo slack key, the guitar is your orchestra. With only six strings, you must somehow manage to play melody, harmony, and bass simultaneously. A carefully chosen tuning is your best asset when attempting this intricate task.

Melody

The melody of your piece will generally be played on the top three strings of your guitar, and occasionally on the lower strings as needed. Try tuning your top strings to pitches that allow easy fingering of scales.

Counterpoint and Chords

This part of your orchestra will be covered by the 2nd, 3rd, and 4th strings, with the emphasis on the 3rd string. Tuning your guitar to common tones of frequently used chords in a piece is valuable. You do not want your left hand restricted to executing harmonic tasks, but free to phrase melodies anywhere on the fingerboard.

Bass

The bass notes will primarily occupy the 4th, 5th, and 6th strings. Once again, tune these strings to the most commonly used bass notes to allow your left hand the freedom to perform melodies. Because bass notes are low pitches, it is important to find the most consonant intervals possible. Have you ever wondered why pianists often play octaves, fifths and fourths in their left hand while playing chords in the right hand? This is because next to the unison (which you cannot play on a piano), the octave is the most consonant interval, followed by the perfect fifth, then the fourth. If you study the overtone series (see Fig 4.3), you'll notice that the octave is the first interval above the fundamental, a fifth is the next interval, and a fourth is the next interval. Because low pitches are heard as fundamentals, they should be spaced at consonant intervals to blend into each other's overtones and to avoid obvious dissonance when they sound together.

Fig. 4.3

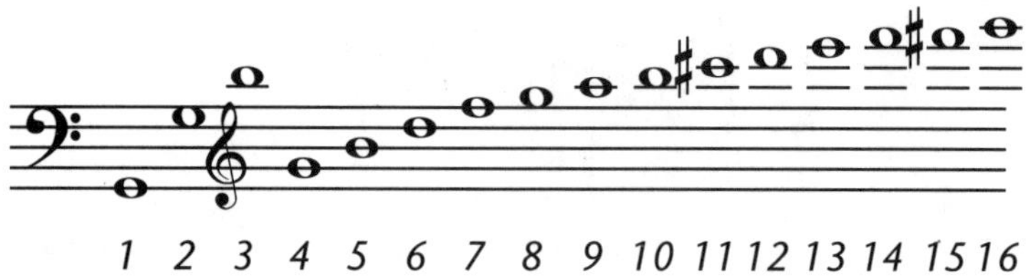

Overtone Series based on a G fundamental

Try the following exercise:

Fig 4.4: In standard tuning, play G♯ on the sixth string and the open fifth string A together.

Fig. 4.4 Track 8

Fig 4.5: In standard tuning, play the open sixth string E and a B on the fifth string together.

Fig. 4.5 Track 9

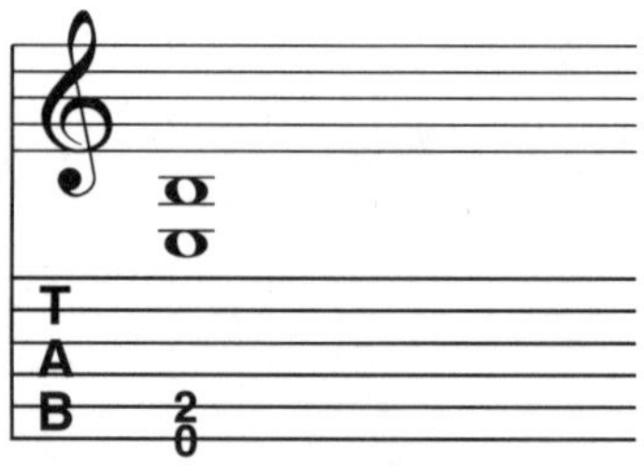

Which sounds consonant? Which is dissonant? Why? The sound produced by the two pitches in Fig 4.5 is considerably more consonant because a perfect fifth is the second most consonant interval while the minor second in example C is the most dissonant interval.

As you can see, the melody, harmony, and bass share common strings. In an orchestra or band, the instruments play in and out of each other's registers as well. You must prioritize the values of these elements when designing your custom tuning. If you like puzzles, this should be a barrel of fun! If you don't like puzzles, imagine the alternative and how much 88 sets of strings and seven gallons of Kona coffee would cost.

Now that you've experimented with different alternate tunings, consider the issue of what else makes your newly-found tuning slack key and not just another altered tuning. Will you apply it to Hawaiian repertoire? Explore it with a recognized slack key master teacher? Remember that there are many issues beyond just the musical ones in this wonderful art form! Now the puzzle really begins.

Chapter 5

G Kilauea Tuning

The G Kilauea tuning (D G C G B E) is a half standard/half slack key tuning. It can simply be described as standard tuning for the upper three strings, with the three lowest pitched strings, E, A, and D, tuned down a whole step to D, G, and C. The G Kilauea tuning falls into the *Ho'opa'a* category of slack key tunings because at least one string needs to be fretted by the left hand to make a chord. I arrived at this tuning by employing the six principles discussed in the previous chapter. Let's revisit this thought process step by step.

Fig. 5.1 Track 10

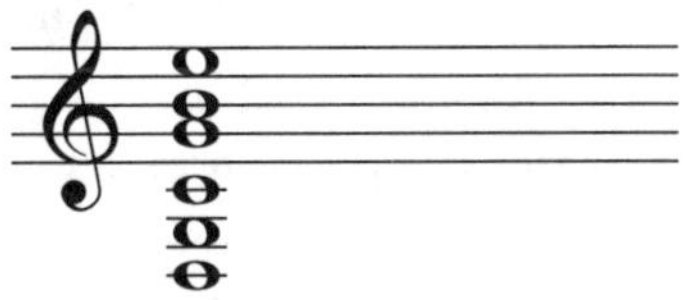

Tension

The three highest pitched strings, G, B, and E, remain at their original tension. The three lowest pitched strings, D, G, and C, are tuned down a whole step but still within a minor third of standard tuning, thus preserving the integrity of the guitar's action and intonation. Theoretically, we could tune the G Kilauea tuning up a half step to D♯, G♯, C♯, G♯, B♯ (C), and E♯ (F) and keep the cumulative tension of the strings close to standard tuning. This should make the action and intonation almost identical to standard tuning.

Key

The G Kilauea tuning works well in G major, G minor, C major, and C minor. The reason it functions in the key of C is because all the same properties exist in this key:

- The melody notes can still be played on the highest pitched strings.
- The 3rd string, G, is also a common tone in the key of C so it can be played as an open string much of the time—G is the 5th of a C chord (I), and the root of a G chord (V).
- The bass notes are all open strings: d=ii, G=V, C=I. The ii chord, d minor, is the relative minor chord to F, which is the IV chord in the key of C. The relative minor chord can function similarly to its related major chord. It has a different character and a different bass note, but many common tones: F, A, and C (the C is the seventh of a D minor chord).

The G Kilauea tuning can be used from a half step lower to a whole step higher and still maintain a playable tension on the guitar; thus producing the following keys:

F♯ or G♭ major

F♯ or G♭ minor

G major

G minor

G♯ or A♭ major

G♯ or A♭ minor

A major

A minor

B major

B minor

C major

C minor

C♯ or Db major

C♯ or Db minor

D major

D minor

Open Strings

In the keys of G major, G minor, C major, and C minor this tuning maximizes the number of playable open strings by providing three for bass notes, D, G, and C, and a common tone on the 3rd string, G.

Melody

If you already play the guitar in standard tuning, the execution of melodies on the top three strings, G, B, and E are made easier by the familiar shapes of chords and scales. Pentatonic, major, and minor scales play comfortably under the left hand.

Counterpoint and Chords

As stated above, the 3rd string, G, is a common tone in both the key of G and the key of C. By allowing you to define harmony without fingering this string, your left hand is free to focus on the phrasing and expression of the melody.

Bass

The three lowest pitched strings, D, G, and C, are the roots of the V, I, and IV chords in the key of G, and the ii, V, and I in the key of C respectively. These are widely used chords in slack key music. D, G and C are each a fourth apart from each other. A fourth is the third most consonant interval (the octave is the first and a perfect fifth is the second most consonant interval). Why then, aren't we tuning the lowest three strings to C, G and D? Aren't perfect fifths and even more consonant than fourths? Obviously, this has been done to great effect already—in fact, this would produce "Keola's C" tuning, as described in Chapter 3. However, as an alternative, there are two reasons to consider tuning the lower three strings to D, G, and C: register and playability. C, G and D span a major ninth—quite a large interval for bass notes in this register. The D is in a register that is used for chording not bass notes, and the C is a major third below the traditional tuning of that string (E). Try tuning your guitar to these pitches then play the D string followed by the C string. Do they sound like they share the same function as bass notes? Also, the playability of strings tuned in perfect fifths is slightly less physically practical on a guitar than when tuned in fourths.

Let's compare the G Kilauea tuning to two popular tunings: the G Taro Patch (D G D G B D) which is the most played slack key tuning, and standard tuning.

The first restriction that comes to mind in the G Taro Patch tuning is that the root pitch of the IV chord, C, is not represented as an open string. This limits the left hand's freedom to play melody, counterpoint, and harmony when the IV chord is used because it must finger the C bass note. The second potential drawback is that by tuning the highest pitched string to D instead of E, scales become more difficult to play because it involves a position change.

Standard tuning is interesting because there are many similarities to the G Kilauea tuning: the top three strings are exactly the same, both tunings have an open string that can function as a common tone, and the three bass strings of both are tuned in fourths which is an ideal interval for bass notes on a guitar. In the key of A using standard tuning, the root pitches of the V (E), I (A), and IV (D) chords are represented on the three lowest pitched strings, the melody can be played with ease on the top three strings, and the high E string is a common tone to the V (E), I (A), and IV (D) chord. Why then would we want to use the G Kilauea tuning when standard tuning seems to possess all the same features? Quite simply, the position of the common tone string that serves a harmonic and contrapuntal function is the determining factor. In standard tuning, the high E strings serves this function because it is the root of the V (E) chord, the fifth of the I (A) chord, and the ninth of the IV (D) chord. This works fine for chording, but if you want to play a melody, this string cannot do both simultaneously. The G Kilauea tuning lowers the tonal center down a whole step from A to G, thus defining the 3rd string, G, as the common tone string. This frees the 1st and 2nd strings to play melodies.

Recognizing that there are many wonderful slack key tunings to explore, I've found it extremely valuable as a performer to focus on one tuning. To be creative, you need to know what the music will sound like before you actually play it on your instrument. Having your guitar in different tunings for every song is not unlike playing a different instrument for each tune. With this in mind, let's investigate some of the qualities of the G Kilauea tuning.

Basic Chords in G Kilauea

Rather than provide a list of every possible voicing of every chord in this tuning (which would be about as helpful as listing all 2,985,984 guitar tunings), here are a few of the more sonically balanced choices in terms voicing and pitch duplication.

Key of G Major

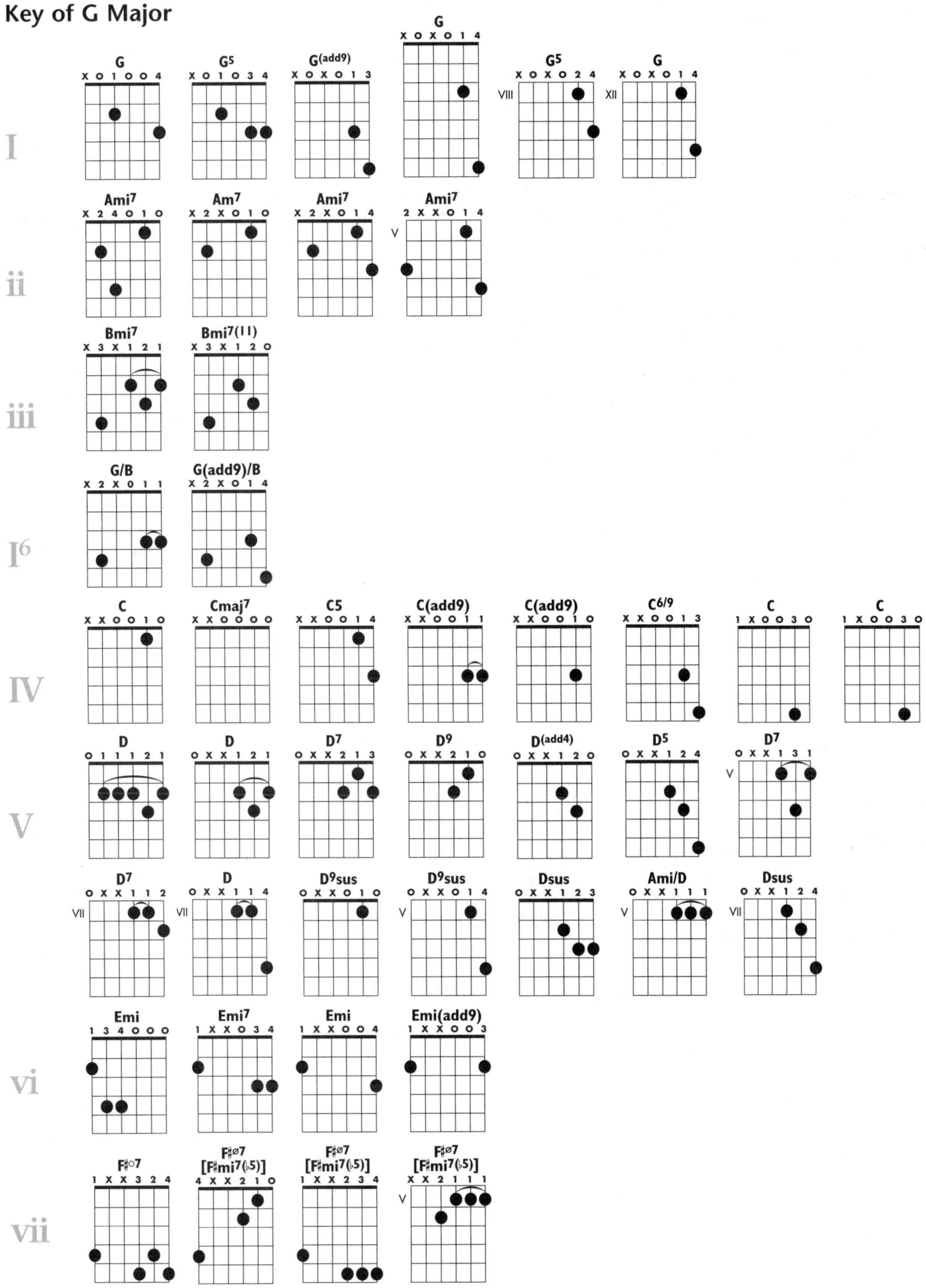

Additional Chords in Key of C Major

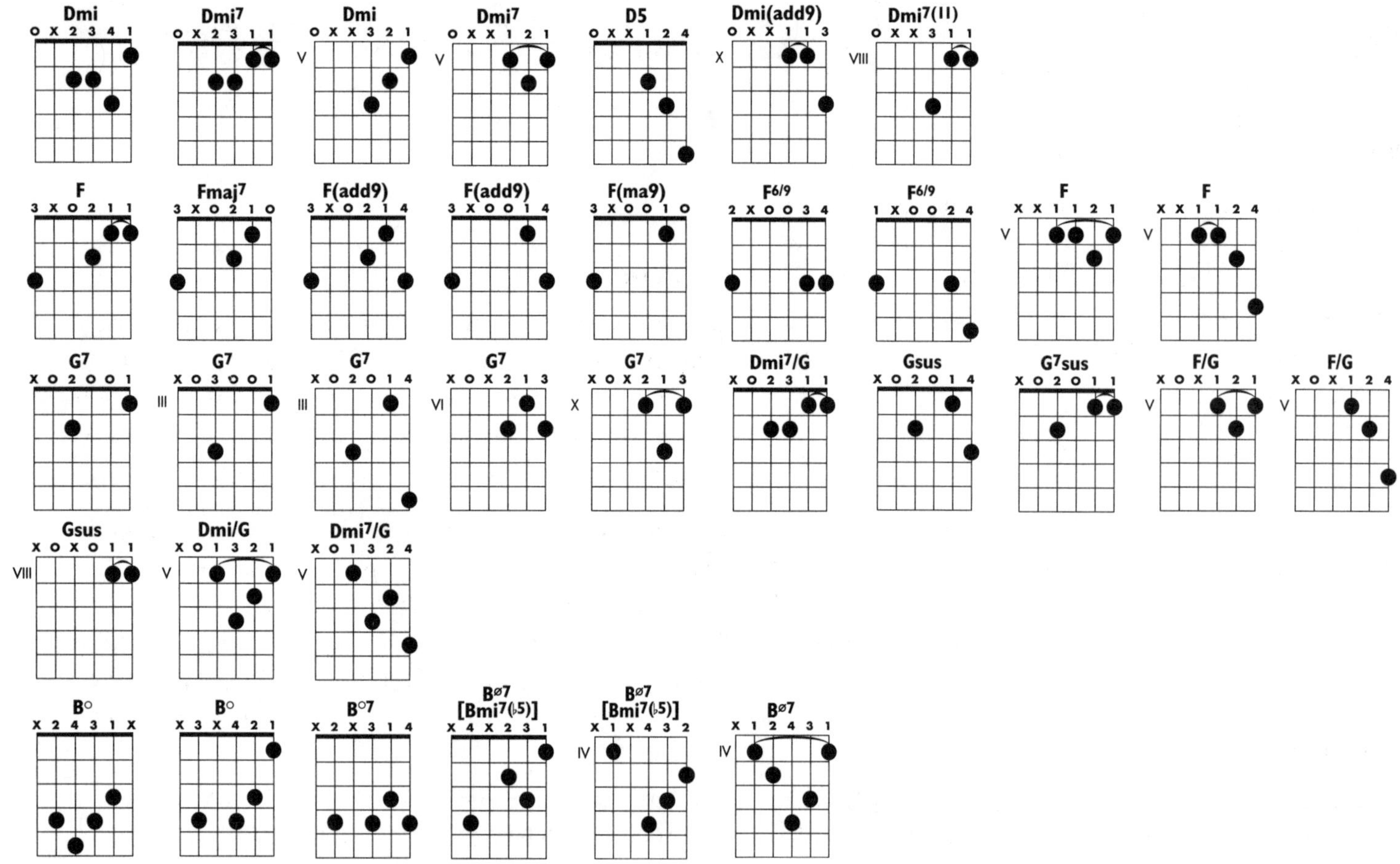

Additional Chords

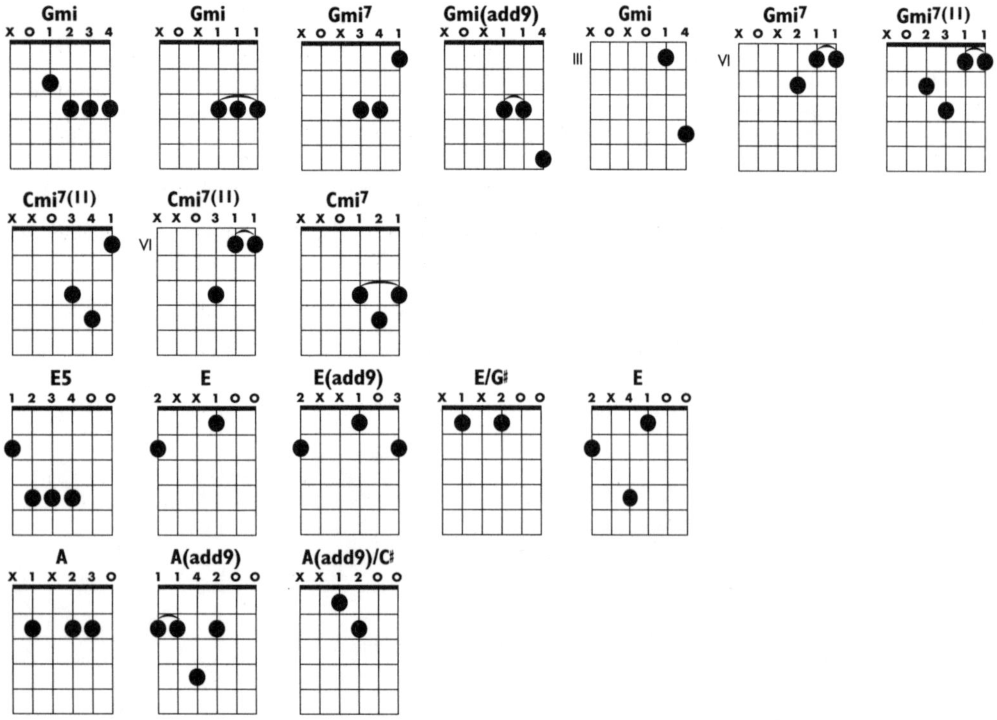

Chapter 6

Creating Your Own Arrangements

Arranging music for solo guitar is a creative and challenging process. Working out an arrangement becomes something of a three dimensional puzzle given the many ways of playing a single passage, the guitar's inherent limitations in register, and the complexity of executing polyphonic textures on the instrument.

As arrangers, we may consider altering tempi, rhythm, harmony, and even the melodic material of the pieces we arrange. To what degree these alterations might take place depends on the situation. We can arrange a piece so that it is barely recognizable to the listener, or almost identical to the original.

When arranging, sometimes we feel our job is complete once we are able to play the melody and harmony at the same time. Even this is not always an easy task. Let's investigate several techniques we can employ to improve upon "two dimensional" melodic/chordal arrangements to make them "three-dimensional"—rich with interest and originality.

Motivic Elements

Weaving an original motivic element through a piece is an effective way to tie a piece together and to lend added cohesion to an arrangement. It gives the listener something to appreciate when the melody is not active, and more importantly, this short compositional element becomes your artistic "signature"—something no other arrangement of that piece would have.

In this arrangement of Hawai'i Aloha, I composed a three-note motive:

Fig. 6.1 Track 11

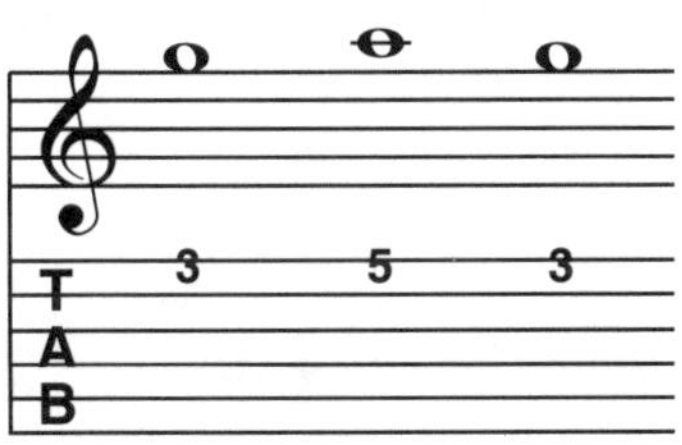

This motive is the theme of the introduction and is also used as counterpoint to the melody throughout the piece. Notice how your ear begins to recognize the subtle appearances of this theme.

Fig. 6.2 Chapter 7.9 ***Hawai'i Aloha,*** *measures 11–14* Track 12

Ostinato

An ostinato is a repeating musical figure. One of the ideas behind an ostinato is that the repetition gradually moves the figure into the background of a listener's consciousness. The listener's attention is then directed to the elements that do change such as the melody.

Imagine taking a plane ride to Hawai'i. You get on the aircraft, fasten your seatbelt, and wait patiently while the flight attendants go through their routine as you taxi to the runway. The tower radios take-off clearance, the jet engines rev to full power, you wonder to yourself, "Am I going to have to listen to these engines roar for hours?" An hour later, you're at cruising altitude completely engrossed in the delicious entrée served to you by that stunningly attractive flight attendant as you fumble though the in-flight magazine. Do you even notice the engines anymore? They seem to disappear into your subconscious as these wonderful experiences occur all around you!

The same phenomenon can happen in music. The repetition of the ostinato draws it into the background, creating a subliminal energy over which a piece can be played.

I used an ostinato in my arrangement of *Pūpū A 'O 'Ewa.* It begins as the introduction and plays though the entire piece with the exclusion of the solo section. In this arrangement, the greatest challenge was keeping the ostinato, melody, and bass going simultaneously.

Fig. 6.3 Chapter 7.8 ***Pūpū A 'O 'Ewa,*** *measures 5–8* Track 13

Pedal Point

This technique was widely used in organ music during the Baroque period. A pedal point is traditionally defined as a low sustained note played on an organ's pedal board over which a passage is played. An inverted pedal point is a high sustained note or group of notes, and an internal pedal point is a sustained musical element in the middle tessatura of a piece. Being that a guitar string doesn't sustain indefinitely, it is often necessary to re-attack pedal points to sustain them through passages.

The following excerpt from *A World Away* is an example of an internal pedal point. The notes that are pedaled are G, C, and G, and they are played in a pattern that could also be considered an ostinato.

Fig. 6.4 Chapter 7.3 ***A World Away,*** *measures 61–64* Track 14

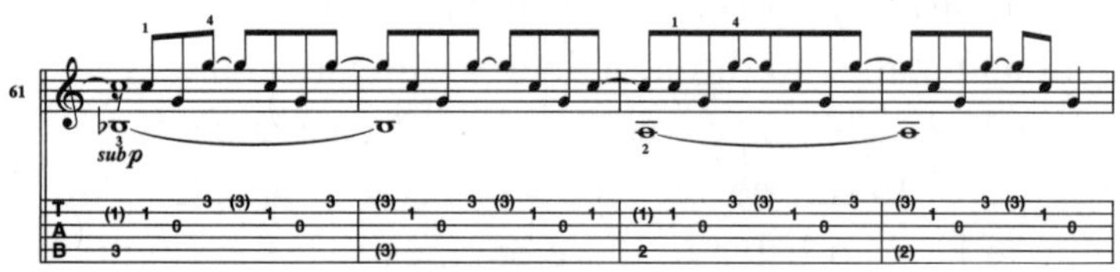

Contrary Motion

This can best be described as two musical elements that move in opposite directions. On a piano, this is not difficult to do. Each hand would play a separate musical element as they move in opposing directions. On a guitar, however, you have one hand (your left hand) defining the majority of the pitches. With this restriction, you really can't exploit this technique with ease, but it can be done.

I used contrary motion in my arrangement of *Hawai'i Pono'i* to create an increased energy towards the end of the phrase.

Fig. 6.5 Chapter 7.10 ***Hawai'i Pono'i,*** *measures 13–15* Track 15

Parallel Motion

Because contrary motion is more difficult to execute on the guitar, parallel motion is one of the most popular harmonization techniques of guitarists. We see this very often in slack key, as many of the most common vamps utilize parallel motion. The most common intervals in this construction are the third, sixth, and tenth.

In *Dreams of Eternity,* I used sixths to highlight the main parts of the melody. The sixths add a richness that bring the melody to the forefront of the musical texture.

Fig. 6.6 Chapter 7.7 ***Dreams of Eternity,*** *measures 1–4* Track 16

The melody of *Allure of the Islands* is treated in much the same way using thirds and sixths.

Fig. 6.7 Chapter 7.12 ***Allure of the Islands,*** *measures 1–4* Track 17

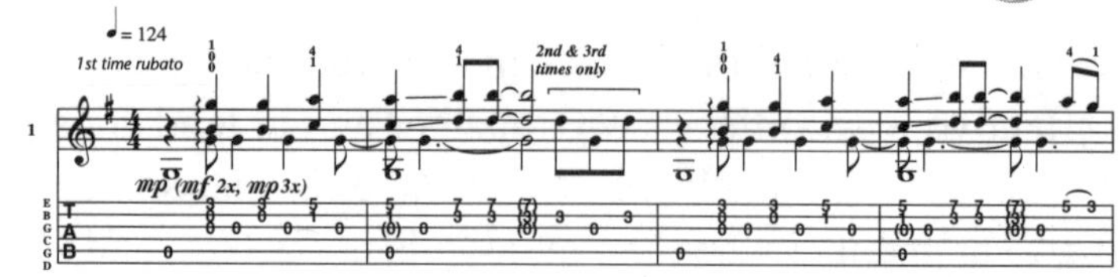

Oblique Motion

When one musical element remains constant in pitch while another moves, this is called oblique motion. This can be effectively used to add interest to an otherwise static melody. I have treated some of the melody in *Hawai'i Pono'i* this way. Notice how an inner voice moves downward in a stepwise motion while the melody remains constant in measures 1–2 and 7–8.

Fig. 6.8a Chapter 7.10 ***Hawai'i Pono'i,*** *measures 1–2* Track 18

Fig. 6.8b Chapter 7.10 ***Hawai'i Pono'i,*** *measures 7–8* Track 19

Reharmonization

Any melody can be harmonized in a number of different ways. Reharmonizing a piece maintains a listener's interest by changing the relationship between the melody and its supporting harmony. An excellent example of this is Steve Sano's arrangement of *Ke Aloha O Ka Haku.* The following example is an excerpt from the first verse of Steve's arrangement, harmonized with the chords found in the original publication of the piece.

Fig. 6.9 Chapter 7.14 ***Ke Aloha O Ka Haku,*** *measures 9–10* Track 20

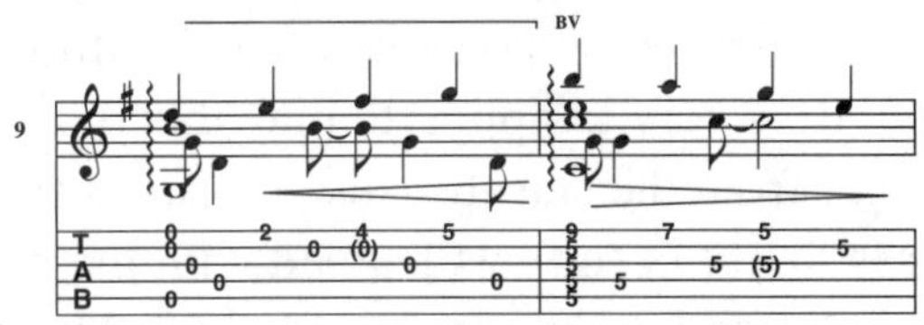

In the second verse, Steve reharmonizes the same melody with a unique set of chords that give this familiar melody a fresh sound.

Fig. 6.10 Chapter 7.14 ***Ke Aloha O Ka Haku,*** *measures 20–21* Track 21

I hope this chapter has opened your mind to that "third dimension" of arranging—that little extra something that will set your music apart. As you become familiar with these techniques and begin to utilize them in your guitar arrangements, you will undoubtedly create a sound that is uniquely personal. Although these tools are in many arranger's "bag of tricks", no two people handle them in exactly the same way.

Chapter 7.1

Song Transcriptions & Mo'olelo

Lia

I wrote this song for my beautiful daughter, Lia, when she was just an infant. In 1997, it was recorded by Canoe Club as a ukulele instrumental on their debut album *Along for the Ride.* This solo slack key version was originally arranged for live performance. I enjoyed playing it so much that I recorded it on *Beyond Blue.*

Performance Notes

When performing this piece, concentrate on keeping a steady, light groove throughout. Proper practicing with a metronome could help you achieve this feel.

In bars 10, 14, and similar passages, I fingered the C bass note on the 5th fret of the 5th string instead of playing the C on the open 4th string. Why would I do this? The purpose for fingering the C bass note is to keep the G bass note in the previous bar from ringing through and creating a muddy sound. Try playing it both ways. You'll notice the resulting clarity of fingering the C bass is worth the extra effort.

The solo section, bars 69–95, begins as a question and answer or "call and response" type of solo. It slowly crescendos to the highest dynamic point of the piece (bars 91–95), then the tension and energy is gradually released in bars 95–96. Bars 91–95 is a great exercise in pull-offs. Practice this section slowly and listen for every note, then gradually increase the tempo as you feel comfortable with the passage. It is very tempting to play this type of passage fast right from the start because it sounds flashy, but the danger is that it never gets learned with the proper precision and clarity necessary for it to sound beautiful.

Bars 97 through the end is where you get a chance to play the guitar with as much finesse and emotion as you can conjure. The trick here is to maintain the subliminal groove throughout this section. It is not easy to keep a steady rhythmic "pocket" at a pianissimo. Ask any drummer!

Lia

Track 22

Daniel Ho

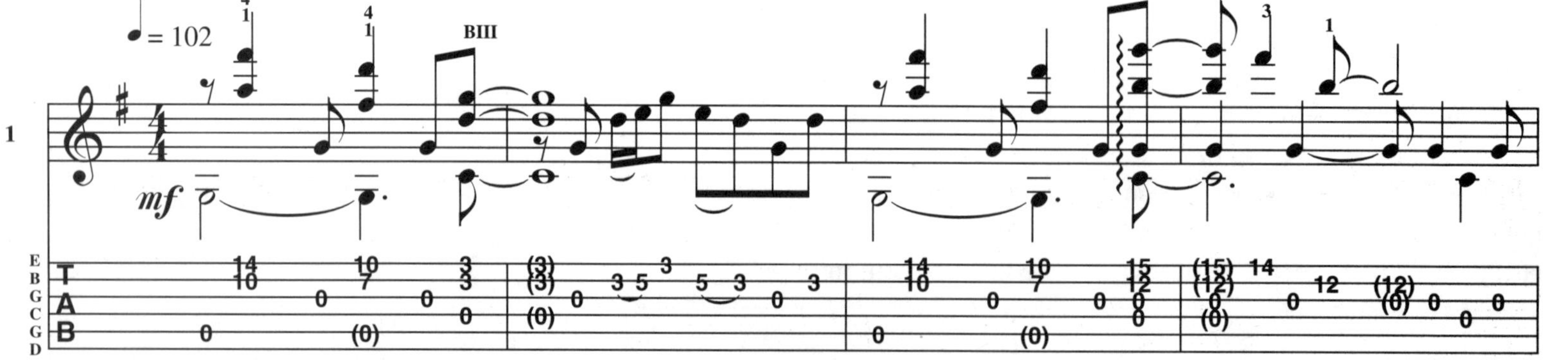

BIII
BVII
mp

BIII
mf
mp
BIII
BIII

41
p
45
49
mp
53
BIII
57
mf

61
65
69
73
77
BIII
T
A
B

81
BIII
85
BIII
f
89
BIII
92
95
BIII
p
BIII
T
A
B

99
103
BIII
108
112
rit.
mf

Chapter 7.2

Song Transcriptions & Mo'olelo

Kumu Mele was also originally recorded as a ukulele instrumental by Canoe Club on *Along for the Ride.* The very talented Lehua Kalima, of Na Leo Pilimehana, lyricized Canoe Club's version and released it on Na Leo's recordings *I Miss You, My Hawaii* (1999) and *Rhythm of the Ocean* (1999) as *Simple as a Sunrise.*

Clearing Storm, Diamond Head

Performance Notes

Although the tempo is very slow, it is probably one of the hardest pieces in this book to play beautifully. You will notice, as you play through it, that many of the harmonies are not common to slack key music. It uses chords outside of the G tonality, for example the Fmaj7 in bar 23, the F^{69} in bars 26 and 28, the E♭maj7 in bars 30 and 32, etc.

The secret to making this piece "sing" is to keep all the melodies and chord changes as legato as possible. This means to hold each pitch or chord as long as you can before letting it go to change positions for the next note or chord.

Kumu Mele

Track 23

(Simple as a Sunrise)

Daniel Ho

BVII
BVII

BV
D.S. al Coda
rit.
CODA
rit.

Chapter 7.3

This piece depicts the joy that surrounds the birth of a couple's first child.

Performance Notes

The syncopations in the choruses (bars 1–16, 46–61, 77–end) usually result in a tendency to rush. The long, lyrical melody of the verse (bars 22–44) as well as the internal pedal point and rhythmic ostinato in the bridge (bars 61–75) generally encourage players to slow down.

The challenge here is to keep a light, bright tempo without rushing or dragging too much. While it is a soloist's prerogative to speed up or slow down as he or she chooses, it should be a conscious decision, not an involuntary response to a piece's idiosyncrasies.

There are many chords that change in rapid succession at times, but they all fall very comfortably under the left hand—an example of how efficient the G Kilauea tuning is in the key of C.

A World Away

Track 24

Daniel Ho

dim.
p
mp
mp

cresc.
mf
f

55
59
sub p
63
cresc.
68
mp
72

77
81
85
89
93
ff

Chapter 7.4

Song Transcriptions & Mo'olelo

A Slack Tide is the point at which the ocean's tide is neither coming or going. I spent much of my youth in Hawai'i on a surfboard, a time in my life when tides played a significant role. In my present existence, tide is nothing more than a laundry detergent...

Waikiki

Performance Notes

This is a funky little slack key tune, and in order to perform it effectively, it is important to understand what characteristics make something "funky".

First of all, you should be able to keep a steady groove going throughout the piece. I noticed as I recorded this piece, that each section seemed to feel better at a different tempo. The chorus (bars 1–9) seemed to feel good a little slower than the funk interlude (bars 9–13), and the verse's tempo (bars 17–25) fell somewhere in between. After minute adjustments to the metronome in my computer (traditional metronomes don't have as fine increments), I found a compromise in tempo that seemed to work for all three sections.

Secondly, the silence between the notes is equally critical to "funkiness" as the notes themselves. This is rather difficult to explain in words as it is more "felt" than "thought". The use of staccatos and ghost notes are essential to achieve this feeling.

Slack Tides

Track 25

Daniel Ho

f
sub p
mp
mf

BVI

43
45
48
51
54

Chapter 7.5

Track 26

Song Transcriptions & Mo'olelo

I thought this *'ukulele* piece would be an interesting instrumental to include. It is an example of how alternate tunings can apply to different instruments. For this piece, tune the C string of your *'ukulele* up to D.

Most of this piece is relatively easy to play. It should be performed in somewhat of an emotionally detached, meditative fashion. The solo ukulele represents the zen spirituality of this traditional Japanese poetic art form.

Bars 25–33, the high point of *Haiku,* is a fabulous exercise for hammer-ons and pull-offs.

Haiku

Track 27

Daniel Ho

rit.

Chapter 7.6

Song Transcriptions & Mo'olelo

The plantation owners of old Hawai'i often hosted elegant parties for their fellow sophisticates and influential Westerners of the day. I imagined watching their graceful ballroom dances as I composed this waltz.

Pineapple Plantation

Performance Notes

Try to keep a gently swinging lilt going throughout. The choruses (bars1–18, 50–67, 99–114, 131–146) should "dance" a bit more than the smooth, legato verses (bars 18–50, 67–99). Notice how well the G Kilauea tuning works in the key of C.

Plantation Waltz

Track 28

Daniel Ho

25
31
37
43
49
55
TAB
BV
mf

BV
dim.
mp
mp

97
BV
103
109
115
121
127
cresc.
f

BV
cresc.
BV

Chapter 7.7

In February and March of 1998, I did a month and a half "bus & truck" tour through the continental U.S. It was during one of those ten hour bus rides that the phrase, *Dreams of Eternity*, came to mind. It was a very sad time for me because I was away from my family for so long, but at the same time, it was fascinating to work with people from all over the world and see places I'd never otherwise visit.

Performance Notes

Much of the melody's main motives are harmonized to add density to their sound and bring them out over the accompanying parts. Listen to the balance of the harmonized melodies, taking care to not let the lower note overpower the higher melody note.

The solo section begins with a "call and response" interaction (bars 55–59). Experiment with creating sounds to differentiate the calls from the answers by using dynamics, ponticello, etc.

Dreams of Eternity

Track 29

Daniel Ho

mp
mf
f
BIII

dim.
mp
to Coda
mf

D. S. al Coda
CODA
rit.

Chapter 7.8

Song Transcriptions & Mo'olelo

Pearly Shells is a popular adaptation of the pre-existing folk melody "Pūpū A'O 'Ewa" from the nineteenth century. "Pūpū A'O 'Ewa" was probably composed "by group effort during a fund-raising campaign for Kahikuokalani Church in 'Ewa."[1] Pearly Shells was copyrighted in 1962 and became one of the most popular Hawaiian songs sung in English. Don Ho (wait, is he related to Daniel?) recorded the song with one verse sung in Hawaiian followed by the English version.

Performance Notes

This arrangement features an ostinato throughout with the exception of the solo section. As the ostinato is considerably more busy than the melody, special attention must be paid to ensure that the melody is the focal point of the arrangement. Try to let the ostinato flow through the piece, disappearing into its own repetition. Make sure you connect and phrase the melody notes as if it were the only thing you were playing. In other words, don't let the ostinato divert your energy and attention away from the most important element—the melody!

[1]*Tater, Elizabeth, "Pūpū A 'O 'Ewa" in Hawaiian Music and Musicians: An Illustrated History, ed. George Kanahele. Honolulu: The University Press of Hawaii, 1979. P. 317.*

Pūpū A 'O 'Ewa

Track 30

(later adapted as Pearly Shells)

Traditional
Arrangement by Daniel Ho

45
mf
49
53
BII
57
60
BV
64
rit.
68

Chapter 7.9

Song Transcriptions & Mo'olelo

The melody to this hymn, now regarded by many as Hawai'i's second anthem, was composed by James McGranahan (1840–1907) as the hymn tune "I Left It All With Jesus." The text was composed by missionary Lorenzo Lyons (1807–1886, also given the name Makua Laiana by the local indigenous population). One of the most enduring and well-known melodies in Hawai'i, Hawai'i Aloha is often sung at the close of concerts in the Islands. The song is regarded as a respectful tribute to the '*aina* (land) and to Hawai'i as "ku'u home," "my home, my native land." In recent years it has also become a political statement among many who support the movement for Hawaiian sovereignty.

Performance Notes

In bars 2, 4, 6, 8, 74, 76, 78, and 80 of the introduction and ending, I chose to finger the C bass note on the 5th string instead of playing the open 4th string. This stopped the G bass note in each of the previous bars from ringing through. The result is a much more clear and consonant sound because the G bass note is not sounding against the C bass note. Try playing it both ways to compare the difference.

Bring out the motivic element with dynamics and phrasing whenever it occurs. It is stated clearly in the introduction and ending, but also subtly interjected in bars 13–14, 17–18, 25–26, 41–42, 59, and 69.

The melodic cross-bar rhythm figure in bars 57–58 should be addressed with the aid of a metronome. The absolute time reference will help you understand the relationship of the syncopations to the beat allowing you to keep a steady tempo through this passage.

Hawai'i Aloha

Track 31

Text composed by Lorenzo Lyons
Melody by James McGranahan
Arrangement by Daniel Ho

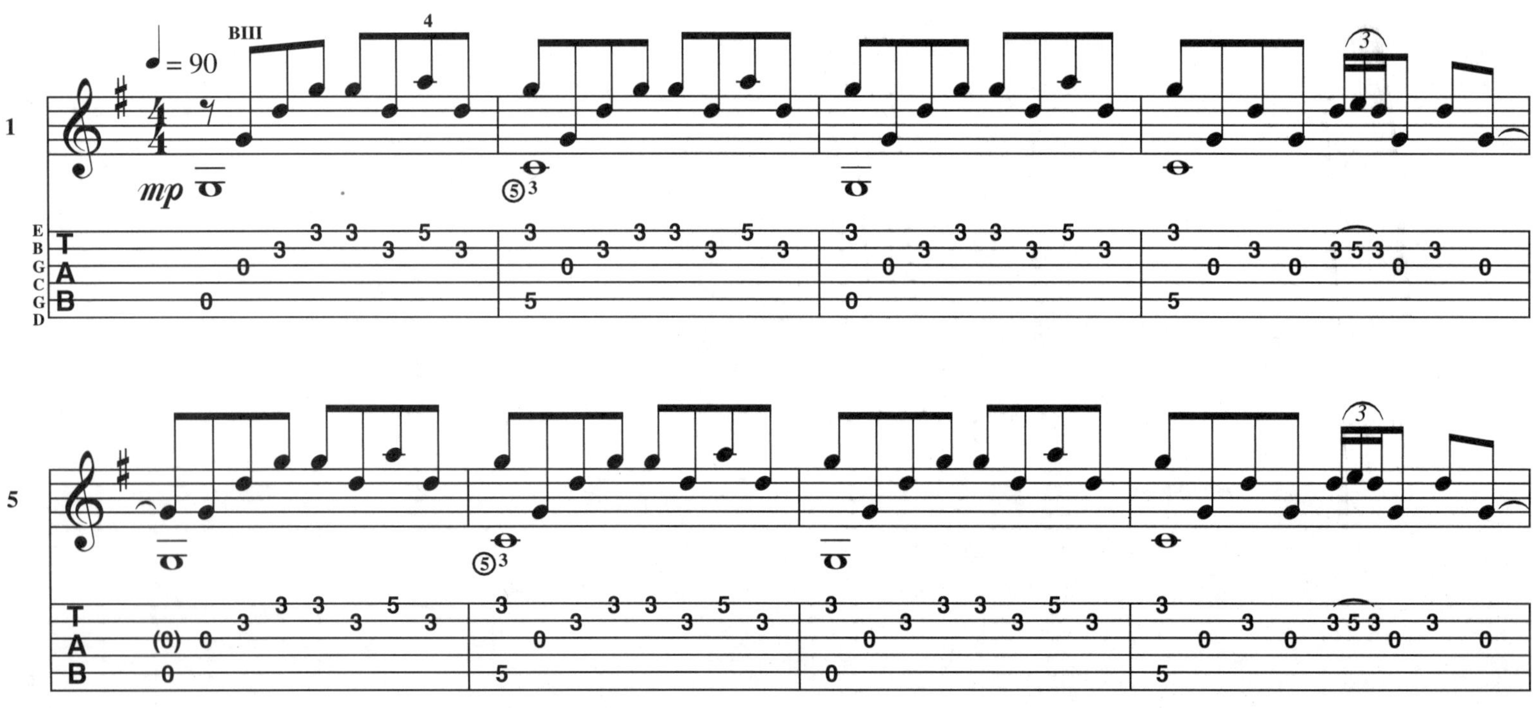

9
13
BII
17
21
BII
BVII
BV
25
mf

29
33
37
BII
BVII
BV
41
dim.
mp
44

48
mf
51
54
cresc.
57
f
cresc.
60

63
66
69
BII
BVII
BV
73
BIII
dim.
77
mp
dim.
pp

Chapter 7.10

Song Transcriptions & Mo'olelo

This was formerly Hawai'i's national anthem and now is the official state song. In 1874, King David Kalākaua authored the text with the intent that it be set to the melody for God Save the King. Henry Berger, bandmaster of His Hawaiian Majesty's Band (later the Royal Hawaiian Military Band, and now the Royal Hawaiian Band) thought that Hawai'i's national anthem deserved its own unique identity and composed the original melody, also in 1874.

Performance Notes

This piece should be played in a moderately slow, regal fashion, as it is Hawai'i's official state song.

Listen for the oblique voice leading in bars 1–3, 7–8, 17–18, and 23–24, parallel motion in bars 3, 5–6, 19, and 21–22, and contrary motion in bars 13, 29, and 37. In these sections, try to phrase the contrapuntal lines as a supporting melody to the primary melody.

King David Kalakaua

Henry Berger

'Iolani Palace

Royal Hawaiian Band

Hawai'i Pono'ī

Track 32

Text by King David Kalākaua
Melody by Henry Berger
Arrangement by Daniel Ho

17
21
mf
26
mp
f
BV
31
mf
mf
36
mp
f
BV
rit.
mf

Chapter 7.11

Queen Lili'uokalani

Unarguably one of the best-known Hawaiian songs, *Aloha 'Oe* was composed in 1877 by Queen Lili'uokalani while she was still a princess. Though widely regarded as a song of farewell, it is in fact, a love song. There are several stories regarding the song's provenance. Perhaps it was inspired by an embrace Princess Lili'uokalani witnessed between her sister, Princess Likelike Cleghorn, and Colonel James Boyd; or perhaps it was an embrace between Colonel Boyd and one of the young ladies at a Maunawili ranch who presented him with a lei. Regardless of its inspiration, *Aloha 'Oe* remains one of the Queen's most enduring and beautiful compositions.

This song has special meaning to me because shortly after my mother passed away in 1972, my father played it on the organ every day. He played it with the emotion displayed by the moving lyrics of the song.

Performance Notes

The primary focus is to keep the melody connected, phrase it with feeling, and prominent over the accompaniment.

Aloha 'Oe

Track 33

Composed by Queen Lili'uokalani
Arrangement by Daniel Ho

9
BV
BIV
BV
BVII
BV
13
17
BII
21
mf
25

28
31
34
BV
1.
BIII
39
2.
BV
43
mp
rit.

Chapter 7.12

Song Transcriptions & Mo'olelo

Island Waterfall

In 1998, I recorded a collaborative album with the popular marine life artist Wyland, entitled *Watercolors. Allure of the Islands* was inspired by a Wyland painting of the same name. We are donating a portion of the proceeds from the sale of *Watercolors* to the Wyland Foundation, whose mission is to promote ocean awareness and conservation.

Performance Notes

The main themes of the melody are harmonized with parallel thirds and sixths. This adds a richness and density that draws attention to them. As you play these passages, make sure the melody is not overpowered by the lower harmony.

The first time through the piece (bars 1–23) can be played rubato, which means freely with give and take in the tempo. You can bring in a steadier tempo at bar 23 and keep it going throughout.

Allure of the Islands

Track 34

Daniel Ho

mp
mp
BV
BVII
BV
BVII
a tempo
mf

29
33
37
41
D.C. al Coda
CODA
45
dim.
rit.
p

Chapter 7.13

Maui Dawn was also inspired by a Wyland painting of the same name. Wyland and I have since recorded three additional albums to benefit the Wyland Foundation: Harmony (Aire 81198), Mysteries (Aire 81298), and Paradise (Aire 80199).

Performance Notes

This piece actually looks a lot harder than it really is. Most of it is played on only the 1st and 2nd strings. Notice in bars 3–4 and 7–8, the E is played on the open 1st string as well as the fingered 2nd string. The beats produced by these slightly detuned pitches combined with the contrasting tones of a fingered E and an open E string create an interesting chorus effect.

The melodic cross-bar rhythm in bars 22–23 should be worked out slowly with a metronome so you can get a feel for where the accents of the melody fall in relation to the beat. If you do not work the passage out this way, the tempo may have a tendency to drift in this section then regain consistency when more obvious rhythmic passages return.

Maui Dawn

Track 35

Daniel Ho

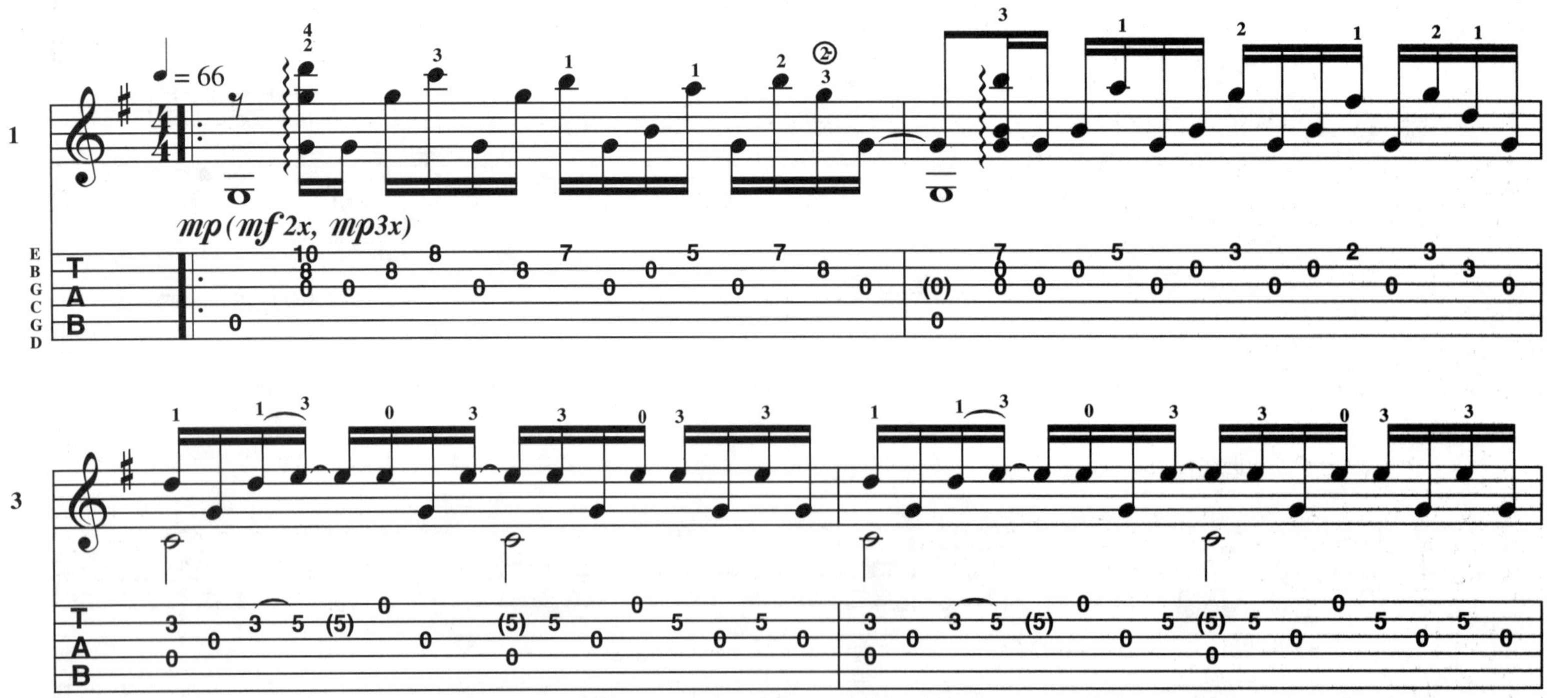

5
7
9
11
mf
p
14
mf
17
p

mp
mf
f
p
dim.
dim.
D. C. al Coda
CODA
dim. e ritard.
pp

Chapter 7.14

In 1893, the Hawaiian monarchy was overthrown by an illegal coup staged by U.S. business interests backed by the U.S. government. The reigning monarch at the time of the overthrow was Queen Lili'uokalani, one of the most prolific and revered of Hawaiian composers. She composed *Ke Aloha O Ka Haku,* which has commonly become known as *"Lili'uokalani's Prayer,"* or *"The Queen's Prayer"* on 22 March 1895, while she was imprisoned in her own palace by her overthrowers. In a poignant twist of irony, the Queen asks the Lord for forgiveness for her overthrowers in the song. The song is dedicated to the Queen's niece, Victoria Ka'iulani.

1Lili'uokalani. Liliuokalani's Prayer and Serenade. Washington D.C.: Sanders & Sayman, 1897

2Lili'uokalani. The Queen's Songbook. Ed. Dorothy Kahananui Gillet & Barbara Barnard Smith. Honolulu: Hui Hānai, 1999.

3 Lili'uokalani. [Music] Ms. MC Liliu, Box 2 and 3, Bernice P. Bishop Museum Archives, Honolulu, and Lili'uokalani. He Buke Mele Hawaii: Hawaiian Songs with Words and Music. Liliuokalani Collection, M-93. Hawai'i State Archives, Honolulu.

Victoria Ka'iulani

Performance Notes

This arrangement consists of a four bar introduction, two verses separated by a short interlude, and a coda, or tag. As mentioned in the chapter on arranging, the first verse has been harmonized in a "conservative" manner. The harmonies for this verse are those in the original published version of the song[1] and in the most recent authoritative volume of the Queen's music[2]. The harmonies in the second verse are more contemporary and feature liberal use of added-tone chords, particularly the added 9th. Also, the melody in bar 8 and bar 19 (third beat D) is the original version composed by the Queen.[3] In all later published versions of this piece, the melody remains on the A for the third beat. The song should be played in a legato style and with great respect—just think of the circumstances under which it was written! Some specific technical issues to think about in playing this arrangement:

•Always be aware of the voicing, i.e., the melody should always be brought out over the accompanimental figures.

•In bars 22 and 26, note the oblique motion in the inner accompanying voice and how it provides a brief counter-melody to the melody's unchanging D above.

•Bar 23 is a deceptive cadence. Remember from chapter 4 that a cadence is a point at which the music comes to rest or resolution. A deceptive cadence is such a point, however, instead of resolving where one expects, it resolves unexpectedly. In this particular case, one would expect bar 22 to resolve in G major—for example one could skip from the end of bar 22 to the downbeat of bar 25. However, instead of the resolution that's expected, bar 23 is a deceptive cadence built on the chords E minor and A9. Treat this bar in a way that will make the listener sit up and take notice! A lot of rubato going into the fermata is very effective here.

• Bars 26 and 27 are a sequence: note that they are the same musical material, but that bar 27 is simply a restatement of bar 26, just a whole-step lower.

• The final three measures should be played with very free rubato—as if there is no time signature.

Ke Aloha O Ka Haku

Track 36

Ke Aloha O Ka Haku (The Lord's Mercy)
Commonly known as *The Queens Prayer* or *Lili'uokalani's Prayer*

Composed by Queen Lili'uokalani
Arrangement by Steve Sano

Tuning: Taro Patch (DGDGBD)

16
mp
BV
19
BV
22
mf
rit.
mf
25
BV
BIII
28
BI
rit.

Chapter 8

Practicing and Performance

Practicing

Practicing is the key to improving your level of playing—and there's a big difference between really practicing a piece, and just playing through it. Practicing is as much a mindset as it is an activity. Practice takes focus, concentration, and a dedication to improving the quality of your work. Remember, amateurs practice until they get it right—professionals practice until they can't get it wrong!

Break down your practice routine into tasks, goals, and time frames that are realistically achievable. It may not be practical to tackle all aspects of a brand new song in one sitting. Rather, work on one section at a time. And within that one section, perhaps there's a particularly tricky passage or crux that requires focused attention. Break down such places in the music into their constituent components: is the challenge tempo? Rhythm? Fingering? Phrasing? Tone production? Identify exactly what it is you need to focus on, and then devise a practice regimen that effectively addresses that one issue.

Remember that slow practice is a great tool—and one that is all-too-often overlooked. It's too easy to mindlessly repeat a passage at a tempo that's too fast to play well. Instead, find that small section that you can easily comprehend, almost memorize. Set your metronome to a painfully slow tempo. Take the first section and play it perfectly three times in a row at this tempo. Set the metronome one click faster and repeat this process until you've reached your desired tempo. Go on to the next section and employ this technique. You will be surprised how quickly you will learn and memorize a piece by doing this. Try not to let mistakes go by unaddressed because this will only teach you to play it wrong! One of the goals of practicing is to take all the thought out of the technical side of the music so you can concentrate on the musical side and make every note count. Music conveys emotion, it tells a story; and you can't do this effectively if you're simply trying to get though a piece without making mistakes.

Performance

There are two things that cure performance anxiety: experience and preparation. Experience simply comes from years and years of being on stage, knowing what works and what doesn't, understanding your audience, and making the most of less than perfect situations. With every successful performance comes a bit of confidence that you can draw upon for future performances. You also begin to build a mental database of things that help or hurt your performance. Distractions like that kukui nut lei that keeps banging your guitar, long sleeves that touch the strings when you play, a belt buckle that scratches your $4,000 instrument, shaky hands from too much coffee before a performance, a bad battery in your guitar pickup, placing your preamp controls too far away from you on stage so you can't adjust your sound easily, not washing your hands after eating that jelly doughnut and getting stuck on the strings, setting your monitor level too high and fighting feedback for an hour and a half, filing your nails too short—these all seem to occur less and less with each passing performance.

Empowering actions such as keeping calm and controlling your anxiety before a performance, clearing your mind of that plummeting stock market that's devastating your net worth by the minute, communicating with your audience effectively, wearing comfortable clothes, being rested, eating right, getting to a gig not "on time" but EARLY— these begin to replace negative distractions that keep you from doing your best on stage.

However, no amount of experience can replace preparation. You can come to a show with your guitar case stuffed full of experience, but if you can't play the music, you'd better have skin as thick as an elephant's to cope with the humiliation ahead. Please don't ask me how I know this. I'm still going to therapy.

Chapter 9

Recording Your Guitar

There are countless ways to capture your guitar performances on"tape"; we use this term loosely as much of today's audio recording is done digitally to hard disk. The following are some considerations when recording your guitar:

Type of Guitar

It's something of a cliché, but always remember the aphorism that it's the player that makes the music, not the instrument! A fine instrument can be a useful tool in optimizing one's skills, but it can't make up for a player's shortcomings, either musical or technical.

Slack key can be played on any type of guitar: steel or nylon string, archtop or flattop, acoustic or electric. No two guitars sound identical—even two of the same model instruments from the same maker can sound dramatically different, so understanding your instrument's individual sonic characteristics is essential. A dark, boomy guitar requires a different microphone, mic placement, and equalization than a bright, thinner sounding instrument.

We are lucky to live in what many call the "golden age of luthiery." Along with the abundance of high quality instruments being built today, there is more written material about guitars and guitar construction available now than ever before. My only caution is to gather your information from reliable sources; respected luthiers and repairfolk, well-regarded publications, and trusted, knowledgeable members of the guitar community. I would caution people about the great amount of misinformation being passed off as "expert knowledge," particularly on the internet—where it's too easy for anyone to be an "expert."

Strings

Dancing Cat Records usually recommends that their artists change their strings two days before a recording session—this provides the advantages of new strings and yet prevents the sound from being too bright. The dirt, oils, and corrosion that build up on older strings make the instrument sound dull and lifeless and reduce sustain. New strings will sqeak louder as you slide your left hand over them, and they will fall out of tune frequently. Sqeaks can be reduced by lightening the pressure on the strings as you change left hand positions, or by finding an alternate way to play the same passage with fewer position changes. Intonation can be helped by stretching the strings after you've changed them, and by tuning your instrument diligently between takes.

Context

Different techniques are used to record a solo guitar versus a guitar that is playing with other instruments. When playing in an ensemble, knowing the density of the track, instrumentation, the guitar's musical function—lead or accompaniment, are all critical factors that help determine the proper treatment of the guitar. If you are recording a solo guitar piece, the goal is to create the richest, fullest sound possible by filling the entire frequency spectrum. If your guitar is playing a duet with a piano, the low-mid frequencies of either the guitar or piano would be compromised to create room for other instruments, depending on the musical function of each instrument. For example, you could boost the guitar's high frequencies which add clarity to the instrument by emphasizing frequencies that are not as strong in the piano. If your guitar is part of a recording that includes hi pitched instruments like shakers, a hi-hat, and/or cymbals, you probably wouldn't boost the hi frequencies of the guitar but find a lower frequency that would complement the already present high end.

Microphone Type

This is a highly subjective topic, and here is my highly subjective opinion. There are two types of microphones I use when recording an acoustic guitar: a condenser microphone (AKG 451) and a tube microphone (AKG C-12). No, I don't endorse AKG, but they sure are good at what they do! Although it's a bit noisier, a tube mic is a great choice for solo guitar. The tube adds a pleasant warmth and detail to the sound. The 451 condenser is a clean and quiet mic. Its small diaphragm produces a presence and attack that helps the guitar get through a track. The difference? The Tube is three times more expensive than the 451.

Microphone Placement

Another subjective area, I'll just share a few ideas that have worked well for me over the years. For solo guitar recording, I generally place the mic about 6 to 12 inches in front of the 12th fret pointing towards the sound hole. The result is a nice balance between the high-end clarity of the strings and the resonant boominess that comes from the sound hole. When I record a guitar that will be used in a track, the density of the track determines the angle of the mic. For an extremely dense track, I aim the mic directly to the 12th fret. This eliminates some of the guitar's fullness and emphasizes the clarity and high-end of the strings. For moderately dense tracks, I aim the mic somewhere between the 12th fret and the soundhole. Experiment with this technique and you will notice a considerable change in tone quality.

Stereo, Mono, & Direct

I almost always record in mono mainly because I don't know where to place the other mic to create a stereo image. Unlike a piano, where there are low strings and high strings to place in a stereo field, a guitar just doesn't have that separation. However, it makes sense to set up an additional mic to capture the ambience of the guitar and blend that in with the main signal. If your guitar has a pickup you can blend a little of the direct signal with the mic sound. The direct sound is much more present and sustains longer. It can sound electronic and heavy in the midrange so I usually just use a touch of it for clarity. When blending the direct signal with the mic, be careful of phase cancellation. This occurs when two soundwaves move in parallel and cancel each other out. Complete phase cancellation is silence. Keeping the direct signal somewhere less than 50% of the mic signal should control this potential problem.

Room

If you are recording in a professional studio with a tuned, soundproofed room, this is not a concern. If you'd like to learn how to get a "professional" sound without spending the money to rent a studio, rest assured, it is not expensive and not difficult. First and foremost, your room must be quiet. This means putting your computer or any noise producing device in a closet or in another room, closing all the windows and doors, turning off your air conditioner or heater, etc. Next, make sure you are not recording too close to any walls. If you have a small room and this in unavoidable, use blankets or insulation panels to cover them. You want to eliminate all short reflections as these quick acoustically untreated reverberations will make your recording sound cheap and boxy. Professional studios tune every board in the room to make the reflections sound just right. Luckily, the guitar is a relatively quiet instrument, and therefore, less affected sonically by a room than, say, a drumset! Imagine recording drums in a tiny room without insulation! Finally, all parallel walls must be tended to. If you live in anything but an avant-garde palatial estate with no parallel walls, this can be accomplished by tearing down your entire house and hiring Frank Gehry. Just kidding! You can either panel the entire room with insulation, or an easier option would be to alternate panels thought the room so the exposed portions of the walls would face insulated panels. This step is not crucial in that very little sound from the guitar will actually make it all the way across the room and back to the microphone. Floors and ceilings can be treated to taste. Carpet is like built in insulation. Hardwood floors can sound wonderful, but if they don't, just throw an area rug under your recording space.

Signal Path

Always have the shortest, cleanest signal path possible. Use the best cables and connectors, and bypass any compressors, limiters, equalizers, and effects processors. The quality of electronics varies from unit to unit so remember—your chain is only as good as its weakest link. I always record completely flat for the simple reason that I can't take it off once I put it on. What if I want less compression? Too late!

Preamp

Of course you can't go wrong with a vintage Neve preamp. But many companies are producing incredibly quiet and powerful preamps for a fraction of the cost. Mackie is one of my favorites—the signal to noise ratio is "studio quality".

Compression

The purpose of compression is to limit the dynamic range of the audio signal. This will make a recording sound smoother and allow for a higher overall level by controlling peaks in the audio. I apply compression only after I have recorded the track so I can tailor the parameters to fit each track individually. There are two kinds of compressors: a single band and a multi band. A single band compressor affects the entire signal when the threshold is exceeded. A multi band compressor divides the frequency spectrum into bands and only compresses the bands that exceed the threshold leaving the other bands unaffected. Either will work well for guitar. Compressors have four basic parameters:

Attack time

This determines how soon the compressor will activate once it recognizes a signal has passed it's threshold. For solo guitar, I use an attack time of about 500 milliseconds to allow for a natural attack to pass before the compressor kicks in.

Threshold

The point at which the compression will activate. I set this function so the compressor is not active all the time. The softer passages are left uncompressed, while the louder passages are affected.

Ratio

The amount of compression applied. For example, a ratio of 1:1 is no compression at all, 2:1 would reduce the level by 50%, 4:1 would reduce the level by 75%. I use a ratio of 3:1 for solo guitar.

Release time: This parameter controls the rate at which the compressor deactivates once the signal falls below the threshold. I usually set this to about 165 milliseconds.

In setting your compressor you should strive to make it sound "invisible". You do not want your audience to hear it activating, deactivating, and affecting the sound.

Equalization

An "eq" is used to control the amount of low, mid, and high frequencies in a recording. There is no formula for setting an eq, because every player, guitar, microphone, room, preamp, and compressor sounds different. There are two types of equalizers: graphic and parametric. A graphic eq can best be compared to the eq on your boombox where each slider controls a different frequency. A fully parametric eq employs such parameters as shelves, high pass filters, low pass filters, and Q—too much to get into for such a short book! The best advice I have is to compare your recording to a CD that is similar in instrumentation and sounds great to your ears. Play with your eq until you get as close as you can to the CD. Don't get discouraged if you can't get it just right, it literally takes years of practice to develop an "ear" for this art. It's no easier than learning to play a guitar!

Reverb

Remember all that effort we put into taking the reflections, reverberations, and sound of the room out of the recording? Here's where we put it back! A reverb effect can put your guitar into a concert hall, church, room, telephone booth, etc., without you leaving the comfort of your home. It's important to think about a reverb effects unit as a musical instrument. Think of it this way—unless you can build your own concert hall in which to record, you will need to depend on your reverb unit to emulate the space for you! Be careful to not use too much effects—you want to feature the guitar and your playing, not the hall you're playing in.

Limiters

A mastering limiter or "brick" limiter is similar to a multi band compressor in that it divides the frequency spectrum into bands and only affects the bands that exceed the threshold. The difference is that the threshold is actually the absolute limit. Any audio that hits the threshold will not exceed it by any ratio as with a compressor, hence the term "brick". Why is this useful? Well, in the digital domain, 0 db is the absolute limit. Any audio that exceeds 0 will be distorted—not in a musical "Jimi Hendrix" way, mind you, but in a harsh, nasty, digital way. So by limiting the loudest points of your audio, the overall level of your recording can be raised.

Appendix

Musical Credits

Lia
Composed by: Daniel Ho
Published by: Little Ming Music (ASCAP) ©1997
From the recording: Beyond Blue (DHC 80900)
Record Label: Daniel Ho Creations (www.DanielHo.com)

Kumu Mele (Simple as a Sunrise)
Composed by: Daniel Ho
Published by: Little Ming Music (ASCAP) ©1997
From the recording: Beyond Blue (DHC 80900)
Record Label: Daniel Ho Creations (www.DanielHo.com)

A World Away
Composed by: Daniel Ho
Published by: Little Ming Music (ASCAP) ©2000
From the recording: Beyond Blue (DHC 80900)
Record Label: Daniel Ho Creations (www.DanielHo.com)

Slack Tides
Composed by: Daniel Ho
Published by: Little Ming Music (ASCAP) ©2000
From the recording: Beyond Blue (DHC 80900)
Record Label: Daniel Ho Creations (www.DanielHo.com)

Haiku
Composed by: Daniel Ho
Published by: Little Ming Music (ASCAP) ©1997
From the recording: Beyond Blue (DHC 80900)
Record Label: Daniel Ho Creations (www.DanielHo.com)

Plantation Waltz
Composed by: Daniel Ho
Published by: Little Ming Music (ASCAP) ©2000
From the recording: Beyond Blue (DHC 80900)
Record Label: Daniel Ho Creations (www.DanielHo.com)

Dreams of Eternity
Composed by: Daniel Ho
Published by: Little Ming Music (ASCAP) ©1998
From the recording: the Voyage Home (Aire 81998)
Record Label: Aire Music (www.AireMusic.com)

Pūpū A'O 'Ewa (later adapted as Pearly Shells)
Traditional melody
Arrangement by: Daniel Ho
From the recording: the Voyage Home (Aire 81998)
Record Label: Aire Music (www.AireMusic.com)

Hawai'i Aloha
Melody composed by: James McGranahan,
text composed by Lorenzo Lyons.
Arrangement by: Daniel Ho
From the recording: the Voyage Home (Aire 81998)
Record Label: Aire Music (www.AireMusic.com)

Hawai'i Pono'i
Melody composed by Henry Berger, text composed by King David Kalākaua
Arrangement by: Daniel Ho
From the recording: the Voyage Home (Aire 81998)
Record Label: Aire Music (www.AireMusic.com)

Aloha 'Oe
Composed by: Queen Lili'uokalani
Arrangement by: Daniel Ho
From the recording: the Voyage Home (Aire 81998)
Record Label: Aire Music (www.AireMusic.com)

Allure of the Islands
Composed by: Daniel Ho
Published by: Little Ming Music (ASCAP) ©1998
From the recording: Watercolors (Aire 86888)
Record Label: Aire Music (www.AireMusic.com)

Maui Dawn
Composed by: Daniel Ho
Published by: Little Ming Music (ASCAP) ©1998
From the recording: Watercolors (Aire 86888)
Record Label: Aire Music (www.AireMusic.com)

Ke Aloha O Ka Haku (The Lord's Mercy)
Commonly known as The Queens Prayer or Lili'uokalani's Prayer
Composed by: Queen Lili'uokalani
Arrangement by: Steve Sano
From the recording: Pu' ukani (DHC 81200)
Record Label: Daniel Ho Creations (www.DanielHo.com)

For current information regarding recordings by Daniel Ho and Steve Sano, please visit: www.DanielHoCreations.com